PRESIDENT'S MALARIA INITIATIVE

Greater Mekong Sub-region

Malaria Operational Plan FY 2016

TABLE OF CONTENTS

ABBREVIATIONS AND ACRONYMS

3DF	Three Diseases Fund
3MDG	Three Millennium Development Goal
ACPR	Adequate clinical and parasitological response
ACT	Artemisinin-based combination therapy
ACTMalaria	Asian Collaborative Training Network for Malaria
ADB	Asian Development Bank
AFRIMS	Armed Forces Research Institute of Medical Sciences
AL	Artemether-lumefantrine
AMTR	Artemisinin Monotherapy Replacement
AP	Atovaquone-proguanil
API	Annual parasite index
AQ	Amodiaquine
A+M	Artesunate and mefloquine
ASEAN	Association of Southeast Asian Nations
BCC	Behavior change communication
BMGF	Bill & Melinda Gates Foundation
BPHWT	Back Pack Health Worker Team
BREMERE	Build Regional Expertise in Medicines Regulation and Enforcement
BVBD	Bureau of Vector-Borne Diseases (Thailand)
CDC	U.S. Centers for Disease Control and Prevention
CMPE	Centre for Malaria, Parasitology, and Entomology (Lao People's Democratic Republic)
CMS	Cambodia Malaria Survey
CMSD	Central Medical Store Depot (Burma)
CNM	National Centre for Parasitology, Entomology, and Malaria (Cambodia)
CQ	Chloroquine
DDF	Department of Drugs and Food (Cambodia)
DFAT	Australia's Department of Foreign Affairs and Trade
DFID	U.K. Department for International Development
DHA-Pip	Dihydroartemisinin-piperaquine
DHIS-2	District Health Information System (2)
DID	Drug Inventory Database
DOT	Directly observed therapy
ERAR	Emergency Response to Artemisinin Resistance
FDA	Food and Drug Administration
FDC	Fixed-Dose Combination
FETP	Field Epidemiology Training Program
G6PD	*Glucose-6-phosphate dehydrogenase*
GHI	Global Health Initiative
Global Fund	Global Fund to Fight AIDS, Tuberculosis, and Malaria
GMS	Greater Mekong Sub-Region
HMIS	Health management information system
IEC	Information, education, communication
IPTp	Intermittent preventive treatment for pregnant women
IPC	Interpersonal Communications

IRS	Indoor residual spraying
ISO	International Organization for Standardization
ITN	Insecticide-treated mosquito net
IVM	Integrated Vector Management
JICA	Japan International Cooperation Agency
Lao PDR	Lao People's Democratic Republic
LLIHN	Long-lasting insecticide-treated hammock net
LLIN	Long-lasting insecticide-treated net
LMI	Lower Mekong Initiative
LMIS	Logistic Management Information System
K13	Kelch 13 propeller
MARC	Myanmar (Burma) Artemisinin Resistance Containment Project
M&E	Monitoring and evaluation
MIP	Malaria in pregnancy
MIS	Malaria indicator survey
MMW	Mobile malaria worker
MOH	Ministry of Health
MOP	Malaria Operational Plan
MOPH	Ministry of Public Health (Thailand)
MPSC	Medical Products Supply Center
MPR	Malaria Program Review
NFM	New Funding Model
NGO	Non-governmental organization
NHQC	National Health Products Quality Control Center
NIH	National Institutes of Health
NIMPE	National Institute for Malariology, Parasitology, and Entomology (Viet Nam)
NMCP	National Malaria Control Program
NSP	National Strategic Plan
OD	Operational district
OR	Operational research
PCR	Polymerase chain reaction
PCVs	Peace Corps Volunteers
PLE	Project for Local Empowerment
PMI	President's Malaria Initiative
PQ	Primaquine
PSI	Population Services International
QA	Quality assurance
QC	Quality control
RAI	Regional Artemisinin Initiative
RBM	Roll Back Malaria
RDMA	Regional Development Mission Asia
RDS	Respondent-driven sampling
RDT	Rapid diagnostic test
SP	Sulfadoxine-pyrimethamine
SSF	Single Stream Funding
TES	Therapeutic efficacy studies

TGA	Therapeutic Goods Administration
TME	Targeted Malaria Elimination
TSG	Technical and Strategic Group
UNFPA	United Nations Population Fund
UNICEF	United Nations Children's Fund
UNOPS	United Nations Office for Project Services
USAID	United States Agency for International Development
USG	United States Government
USP	United States Pharmacopeia
VBDC	Vector-borne Disease Control Program (Burma)
VMW	Village Malaria Worker
WPRO	Western Pacific Regional Office
WHO	World Health Organization

I.   EXECUTIVE SUMMARY

When it was launched in 2005, the goal of the President's Malaria Initiative (PMI) was to reduce malaria-related mortality by 50% across 15 high-burden countries in sub-Saharan Africa through a rapid scale-up of four proven and highly effective malaria prevention and treatment measures: insecticide-treated mosquito nets (ITNs); indoor residual spraying (IRS); accurate diagnosis and prompt treatment with artemisinin-based combination therapies (ACTs); and intermittent preventive treatment of pregnant women (IPTp). With the passage of the Tom Lantos and Henry J. Hyde Global Leadership against HIV/AIDS, Tuberculosis, and Malaria Act in 2008, PMI developed a U.S. Government Malaria Strategy for 2009–2014. This strategy included a long-term vision for malaria control in which sustained high coverage with malaria prevention and treatment interventions would progressively lead to malaria-free zones in Africa, with the ultimate goal of worldwide malaria eradication by 2040-2050. Consistent with this strategy and the increase in annual appropriations supporting PMI, four new sub-Saharan African countries and one regional program in the Greater Mekong Subregion of Southeast Asia were added in 2011. The contributions of PMI, together with those of other partners, have led to dramatic improvements in the coverage of malaria control interventions in PMI-supported countries, and all 15 original countries have documented substantial declines in all-cause mortality rates among children less than five years of age.

In 2015, PMI launched the next six-year strategy, setting forth a bold and ambitious goal and objectives. The PMI Strategy for 2015-2020 takes into account the progress over the past decade and the new challenges that have arisen. Malaria prevention and control remains a major U.S. foreign assistance objective and PMI's Strategy fully aligns with the U.S. Government's vision of ending preventable child and maternal deaths and ending extreme poverty. It is also in line with the goals articulated in the RBM Partnership's second generation global malaria action plan, *Action and Investment to defeat Malaria (AIM) 2016-2030: for a Malaria-Free World* and WHO's updated *Global Technical Strategy: 2016-2030.* Under the PMI Strategy 2015-2020, the U.S. Government's goal is to work with PMI-supported countries and partners to further reduce malaria deaths and substantially decrease malaria morbidity, towards the long-term goal of elimination.

In 2011, PMI support extended to the Greater Mekong Sub-region (GMS), which is made up of six countries: Burma, Cambodia, China (Yunnan Province), Lao People's Democratic Republic (PDR), Thailand, and Viet Nam. This FY 2016 GMS Malaria Operational Plan (MOP) presents detailed implementation plans for Burma, Cambodia, and Thailand/Regional which includes the Lao People's Democratic Republic (Lao PDR) and Viet Nam.

Although considerable progress has been made in malaria control in the GMS during the past 10 years, malaria remains a major concern for the international community, ministries of health, and the people of the region. This is due primarily to the development and possible spread of resistance to artemisinin drugs, the principal component of the combination therapies for malaria that now are the first-line treatment for malaria throughout the GMS and the world. *Plasmodium falciparum* resistance to artemisinin drugs was first confirmed in western Cambodia; failures in artemisinin-based combination therapy (ACT) have been reported from multiple sites on the Thai-Cambodian border; and an early warning sign of artemisinin resistance — prolongation of parasite clearance times — has been reported from the Thailand-Burma, Burma-China borders, southern Viet Nam, and southern Lao PDR.

The USG has supported malaria control efforts in the GMS since 2000. These regional efforts have focused on antimalarial drug resistance monitoring and drug quality surveillance. All GMS countries have received Global Fund to Fight AIDS, Tuberculosis, and Malaria (Global Fund) support. The other major sources of funding for malaria in the region are the multi-donor initiative, the Three Millennium Development Goal Fund, formerly known as the Three Diseases Fund, the Australian Department of Foreign Affairs and Trade, and the Bill and Melinda Gates Foundation. In addition, the Global Fund has launched a 3-year $100 million Regional Artemisinin Initiative to reduce malaria transmission and respond to resistance in GMS countries.

The FY 2016 PMI Malaria Operational Plan for the GMS was developed with the Regional Development Mission for Asia (RDMA), and Burma and Cambodia USAID Missions during a planning visit in April-May 2015 by representatives from USAID, the Centers for Disease Control and Prevention, and the national malaria control programs of Burma, Thailand, and Cambodia, with the participation of other major partners working on malaria in the area.

The FY 2016 Malaria Operational Plan supports regional/cross-cutting activities, such as surveillance for antimalarial drug resistance and antimalarial drug quality assurance, and malaria prevention and control activities to reduce malaria transmission in geographically focused cross-border areas with emerging artemisinin resistance. Original key cross-border focus areas were centered on Tanintharyi-Ranong border areas of Burma and Thailand and the Trat/Chanthaburi-Pailin border areas of Thailand and Cambodia. Subsequently, PMI expanded malaria control activities to other target areas within the three focus countries where there was a high burden of malaria and evidence of confirmed or emerging artemisinin resistance including Kayin and southern Rakhine states in Burma; certain operational districts in Cambodia bordering Thailand, Laos and Viet Nam; and Tak and Kanchanaburi provinces in Thailand. PMI will also consider emergency assistance, including commodity support and technical assistance for surveillance, case management, and behavior change communication (BCC) in other GMS areas threatened by artemisinin resistance. The proposed FY 2016 PMI activities are in line with the national malaria control program strategies of the six countries and are intended to complement ongoing Global Fund malaria grants and contributions from other donors.

The proposed FY 2016 PMI budget for the GMS is $16.5 million. This budget is allocated across countries as follows: $9 million to Burma, $4.5 million to Cambodia, and $3 million to Thailand, Lao PDR, and Viet Nam. PMI will support the following intervention areas with these funds:

Vector control: Malaria transmission in the GMS is closely associated with two malaria vectors that inhabit the forest and forest fringe, *Anopheles dirus* and *An. minimus*. Countries have made progress in monitoring vector distribution and insecticide resistance, which is not a major problem in the GMS area. Most studies suggest that insecticide-treated nets (ITNs) provide protection even with significant outdoor and early evening biting. There is a strong culture of bed net use in the GMS and net ownership is quite high, especially in Burma and Cambodia, but many of those nets are untreated. Considerable numbers of long-lasting ITNs targeted for townships along the Burma-Thailand border and the Thailand-Cambodia border are included in their respective Global Fund grants. With FY 2014 and FY 2015 funding, PMI procured approximately 823,000 and 423,000 long-lasting insecticide-treated nets (LLINs), respectively, to fill gaps in Global Fund grants in the cross-border PMI focus areas and developed innovative BCC approaches to improve LLIN use among vulnerable migrant and mobile populations.

With FY 2016 funding, PMI will procure approximately 607,000 LLINs and hammock nets for migrant and vulnerable populations in targeted focus areas. PMI will also provide support for entomological services and training in the region, in response to the changing vector ecology. Indoor residual spraying (IRS) is mostly limited to outbreak response and focal control and is not a key activity in national malaria control strategies in the GMS with the exception of Thailand. Therefore, no PMI funds will be targeted for IRS in the sub-region.

Malaria in pregnancy: While intermittent preventive treatment for pregnant women (IPTp) is not part of national policies for any country in the sub-region, PMI will support promotion of universal LLIN coverage and prompt diagnosis and treatment of clinical cases of malaria in pregnant women as they remain a vulnerable group in the region. PMI supported a rapid assessment of malaria in pregnancy to identify programmatic areas for strengthening in Burma, Cambodia, and Thailand and will complete the assessment in Lao PDR in 2015. With FY 2014 and FY 2015 funding, PMI is building on the assessment findings and recommendations to ensure all GMS national programs have updated policies and guidelines. In FY 2016, PMI will support training and supervision of facility staff and updating materials to strengthen malaria case management and prevention activities provided through antenatal clinics in Burma and Cambodia.

Case management: In all countries making up the GMS, diagnosis of malaria is based on laboratory tests with microscopy or rapid diagnostic tests (RDTs). Although all countries in the sub-region recommend ACTs as the first-line treatment of *Plasmodium falciparum* infections, artemisinin resistance has been confirmed on the Thai-Cambodian border and early evidence of emerging resistance has been reported from several other sites in the sub-region. Case management of malaria in the GMS is further complicated by the fact that *P. vivax* and *P. falciparum* are both relatively common. Chloroquine is the drug of choice for the treatment of *P. vivax* infections except for Cambodia and Lao PDR, although reports of *P. vivax* resistance to chloroquine are emerging from the sub-region. Another problem in the GMS is the widespread availability of counterfeit and substandard antimalarial drugs, especially artemisinin drugs, and artemisinin monotherapy. With USG support, considerable progress has been made in recent years in establishing effective drug quality monitoring in the sub-region but, to date, engagement with China has been limited. With FY 2014 and FY 2015 funding, PMI has supported training of community health and malaria volunteers and health facility staff in Burma, Cambodia, and Thailand in malaria case management including diagnostic testing.

The majority of RDT and ACT needs in Burma, Cambodia, and Thailand are anticipated to be met by those countries' Global Fund grants through 2016 when the Global Fund malaria grants in Burma and Thailand will end. With FY 2016 funding, PMI will procure small quantities of RDTs to fill gaps and strengthen laboratory capacity in targeted focus areas. PMI will also procure ACT treatments to fill any gaps in Burma and Cambodia and respond to urgent needs in the region. Because of concerns about the quality of malaria diagnosis and treatment in targeted border areas, PMI will support in-service training and quality assurance of the parasitological diagnosis of malaria. In addition, PMI will continue to support drug quality assurance efforts by helping the national pharmaceutical reference laboratories in Burma, Cambodia, and Thailand achieve international standards of accreditation.

Behavior change communications (BCC): PMI will continue to provide technical support to national programs to facilitate development and use of effective communication strategies and appropriate BCC approaches. As countries move from malaria control to elimination, BCC interventions will need to be more tailored and targeted for hard-to-reach populations that remain at risk. PMI supports integration of BCC activities in the delivery of malaria services (e.g., distribution of LLINs and case management). A multi-pronged, comprehensive approach for BCC interventions will be emphasized to sustain community involvement, support promotion of healthy behaviors, and reduce risk-taking in the context of malaria exposure. With FY 2016 funding, PMI will support development of effective BCC approaches for elimination in targeted areas of Cambodia. In Burma, with FY 2016 funding, PMI will support efforts to standardize and harmonize key BCC materials and messages at the community level. In Thailand, PMI will continue to support integration of BCC activities in the delivery of malaria prevention and control services.

Monitoring and evaluation (M&E), surveillance, and operational research: The quality of malaria case detection and reporting systems varies widely within the GMS. In the context of malaria elimination, accurate and timely data are essential to identify cases, mount a timely response, inform policy decisions, and focus resources towards outbreak areas or in geographical regions harboring resistant malaria strains. USG funding for M&E during the past several years has focused on building a regional malaria M&E framework, updating national M&E plans, providing technical assistance for surveys, and capacity development at the national level. With FY 2014 and FY 2015 funding, PMI is supporting strengthening of surveillance systems in Burma and Lao PDR, providing technical assistance for national surveys in Cambodia and Burma, strengthening routine surveillance systems, and collecting routine surveillance and survey data in PMI focus areas.

With FY 2016 funding, PMI will focus efforts on targeted areas to implement systems and practices to foster timely collection of quality surveillance data. At the national level, PMI will provide technical support to all national malaria control programs on their national M&E plans, through support for national/ sub-national malaria surveys, and build M&E capacity within their national programs. In Cambodia and Burma where most patients seek care in the private sector, PMI will continue to strengthen collection of malaria data from private providers. PMI will continue to support drug resistance monitoring at 46 sites (alternating every other year) in all six GMS countries. Entomological surveillance will focus geographically on target and cross-border areas and operational research will continue to identify vector control interventions appropriate for outdoor transmission settings and improving case management.

II.   INTRODUCTION

1. *Greater Mekong Sub-region Malaria Operational Plan*

When it was launched in 2005, the goal of PMI was to reduce malaria-related mortality by 50% across 15 high-burden countries in sub-Saharan Africa through a rapid scale-up of four proven and highly effective malaria prevention and treatment measures: insecticide-treated mosquito nets (ITNs); indoor residual spraying (IRS); accurate diagnosis and prompt treatment with artemisinin-based combination therapies (ACTs); and intermittent preventive treatment of pregnant women (IPTp). With the passage of the Tom Lantos and Henry J. Hyde Global Leadership against HIV/AIDS, Tuberculosis, and Malaria Act in 2008, PMI developed a U.S. Government Malaria Strategy for 2009–2014. This strategy included a long-term vision for malaria control in which sustained high coverage with malaria prevention and treatment interventions would progressively lead to malaria-free zones in Africa, with the ultimate goal of worldwide malaria eradication by 2040-2050. Consistent with this strategy and the increase in annual appropriations supporting PMI, four new sub-Saharan African countries and one regional program in the Greater Mekong Subregion of Southeast Asia were added in 2011. The contributions of PMI, together with those of other partners, have led to dramatic improvements in the coverage of malaria control interventions in PMI-supported countries, and all 15 original countries have documented substantial declines in all-cause mortality rates among children less than five years of age.

In 2015, PMI launched the next six-year strategy, setting forth a bold and ambitious goal and objectives. The PMI Strategy for 2015-2020 takes into account the progress over the past decade and the new challenges that have arisen. Malaria prevention and control remains a major U.S. foreign assistance objective and PMI's Strategy fully aligns with the U.S. Government's vision of ending preventable child and maternal deaths and ending extreme poverty. It is also in line with the goals articulated in the RBM Partnership's second generation global malaria action plan, Action and Investment to defeat Malaria (AIM) 2016-2030: for a Malaria-Free World and WHO's updated Global Technical Strategy: 2016-2030. Under the PMI Strategy 2015-2020, the U.S. Government's goal is to work with PMI-supported countries and partners to further reduce malaria deaths and substantially decrease malaria morbidity, towards the long-term goal of elimination.

In 2011, PMI support extended to the Greater Mekong Sub-region (GMS), which is made up of six countries: Burma, Cambodia, China (Yunnan Province), Lao People's Democratic Republic (PDR), Thailand, and Viet Nam. This FY 2016 GMS Malaria Operational Plan (MOP) presents detailed implementation plans for Burma, Cambodia and Thailand/Regional which includes Lao PDR and Viet Nam.

The MOPs were developed in consultation with the Burma, Thailand, and Cambodian National Malaria Control Programs (NMCPs) and with the input of multiple national and international partners involved with malaria prevention and control in the sub-region. The activities that PMI is proposing to support with FY 2016 funding contribute to the countries' national malaria control/elimination strategies and plans, and build on malaria investments made by the United States Government (USG) in the sub-region since 2000.

11

PMI's GMS program differs from its support to malaria programs in Africa both in its regional focus and its primary goal of responding to artemisinin resistance by eliminating *Plasmodium falciparum*. PMI recognizes the original intent of its engagement in the region was principally due to the emergence of artemisinin resistance, which could undermine the tremendous progress made in the reduction of morbidity and mortality in Africa. While initial PMI priority intervention areas focused on specific border areas between Thailand, Cambodia, and Burma, more recent evidence from the network of therapeutic efficacy studies (TES) and research suggests that artemisinin resistance is more widespread than previously thought. In line with regional goals, PMI has shifted its approach to support regional elimination of *P. falciparum* recognizing that this is the best and most sustainable approach to addressing multi-drug resistance.

The FY 2016 MOPs for the GMS support both regional/cross-cutting activities, such as surveillance for antimalarial drug resistance and regional capacity building, as well as targeted malaria control and elimination activities with a country-specific focus through bilateral funding, particularly in Cambodia, Burma, and Thailand (for detailed discussion of PMI's strategy and objectives, see section on PMI goal, objectives, strategic areas, and key indicators). Support for control and elimination activities in the GMS includes distributing long-lasting insecticide-treated nets (LLINs) to protect against indoor biting mosquitoes; improving access to rapid diagnosis and effective treatment of malaria cases in the public and private sectors; promoting behavior change communication (BCC) to reinforce use of personal protection measures and appropriate care-seeking; strengthening routine malaria surveillance systems; supporting entomological monitoring to monitor for insecticide resistance; and identifying operational research to improve program implementation and test the feasibility of new tools.

Regional, cross-cutting activities will benefit all six countries making up the GMS, depending on access and other sources of funding. Particularly with country-specific bilateral activities in Burma and Cambodia, it will be important to ensure that activities and lessons learned are coordinated and shared as much as possible for maximum impact. Given the heterogeneous burden of malaria and the presence of artemisinin resistance in the GMS, initial focus of the country-specific, community-based intervention activities was centered on the Trat/Chanthaburi-Pailin border areas of Thailand and Cambodia. Artemisinin resistance has now been detected along the border areas of Burma and Thailand, southern Viet Nam, and southern Laos bordering Thailand and Cambodia. Therefore, PMI has expanded malaria control/elimination activities to other target areas within the three focus countries where there is evidence of confirmed or emerging artemisinin resistance including: Tanintharyi, Kayin, Rakhine, Kayah, and Bago states in Burma; Tak, Ranong, and Kanchanaburi provinces in Thailand; and several operational districts in West, North, and East of Cambodia bordering Thailand, Lao PDR, and Viet Nam. In support of NMCP strategies and coordination with other donor efforts, PMI's commodity investments will be focused on filling gaps that are not otherwise filled by country or Global Fund support, with a specific targeting of mobile and migrant workers.

This document reviews the current status of malaria control policies and interventions in the GMS, describes progress to date, identifies challenges and unmet needs if the targets of the

NMCPs and PMI are to be achieved, and provides a description of planned activities with FY 2016 funding.

2. *Malaria situation in the GMS*

Malaria control and elimination in the GMS faces many challenges different from those in the African context. The GMS is considered the epicenter of antimalarial drug resistance starting with chloroquine (CQ) resistance in the late 1950s, followed by resistance to sulfadoxine-pyrimethamine (SP), mefloquine, and decreased sensitivity to quinine. Resistance to these antimalarials eventually spread or developed *de novo* throughout the region and globally. The emergence of artemisinin resistance along the Thai-Cambodia border in the early 2000s, the same area where chloroquine resistance emerged 50 years earlier and its subsequent emergence and spread to other parts of the GMS, Africa, and beyond, is of great concern as ACTs are the last remaining simple, efficacious, and well-tolerated treatment for *P. falciparum*.

WHO has classified geographical areas into three tiers of artemisinin resistance (Figure 1):

- Tier 1: Areas where there is credible evidence of artemisinin resistance
- Tier 2: Areas with significant inflows of people from tier 1 areas, including those immediately bordering tier 1
- Tier 3: Areas with no evidence of artemisinin resistance and limited contact with tier 1 areas.

Figure 1. Map of suspected and confirmed areas with artemisinin resistance in the Greater Mekong Sub-region

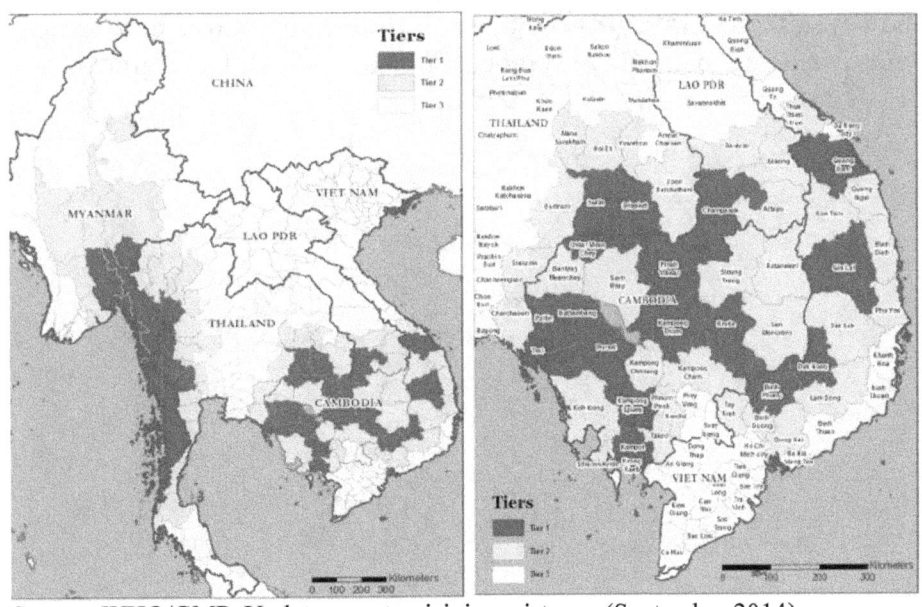

Source: WHO/GMP, Update on artemisinin resistance (September 2014)

According to the WHO, the working definition of partial artemisinin resistance was developed based on observations from routine therapeutic efficacy studies of ACTs, clinical trials of artesunate monotherapy, and mutations in the K13-propeller sequence:

Suspected partial artemisinin resistance is defined as:
- ≥ 5% of patients carrying K13 resistance-associated mutations; or
- ≥ 10% of patients with persistent parasitemia by microscopy on Day 3 after treatment with ACT or artesunate monotherapy; or
- ≥ 10% of patients with a parasite clearance half-life of ≥ 5 hours after treatment with ACT or artesunate monotherapy.

Confirmed artemisinin resistance is defined as: ≥ 5% of patients carrying K13 resistance-associated mutations, all of whom have been found, after treatment with ACT or artesunate monotherapy, to have either persistent parasitemia by microscopy on Day 3, or a parasite clearance half-life of ≥ 5 hours.

Beyond drug resistance, NMCPs in the GMS face several related challenges including variable and largely unquantified delivery of malaria services in the private sector; improved, but continuing infiltration of substandard medications due to weak regulation and enforcement; inadequate systems to ensure service delivery to populations most at risk, particularly mobile and migrant workers; and civil strife and occasional cross-border conflicts. As malaria burden continues to decrease in the GMS and become more heterogeneous, traditional one-size-fits-all approaches may not be relevant or effective in these settings.

National treatment guidelines and policies of the countries comprising the GMS are listed in Table 1.[1] All countries in the GMS now recommend ACTs for first-line treatment of *P. falciparum;* however, treatment regimens and drug choice differ from country to country and pose a particular challenge to ensure adherence among cross-border migrants.

---

[1] Malaria in the Greater Mekong Sub-region: Regional and Country Profiles. WHO 2010

Table 1. National treatment guidelines, strategies, and policies in the GMS

	Burma	Cambodia	China	Lao PDR	Thailand	Viet Nam
Year in which treatment guidelines were most recently updated	**2012**	**2014**	**2009**	**2013**	**2014**	**2009**
First-line treatment for *P. falciparum*	AL; A+M; DHA-Pip	A+M (FDC) (Pailin, Battambang, Oddar Meanchey, Preah Vihear, Pursat); DHA-Pip (all other provinces);	DHA-Pip; AS+AQ; AS+ naphthoquine; AS+PIP (Pip monotherapy as chemo-prophylaxis)	AL (Artemether 20 mg + Lumefantrine 120 mg) based on patient weight or age group for 3 days	A+M	DHA-Pip
Anti-gametocytocidal treatment	45 mg PQ	15 mg PQ given on Day 0 (if G6PD status is known)		45 mg PQ	30 mg PQ	30 mg PQ
First-line treatment for *P. vivax*	CQ+PQ (14d)	DHA-Pip + PQ (0.25 mg/kg x 14 days OR 0.75 mg/kg weekly x 8 weeks)	CQ+PQ (180 mg over 8d)	AL	CQ+PQ (14d)	CQ+PQ (14d)
Treatment of malaria in pregnancy	1st Trimester: Quinine 10mg/kg (7days) + Clindamycin 2nd and 3rd Trimesters: AL (3 days) or A+M (3 days) or DHA-Pip (3 days) + Clindamycin	1st Trimester: Quinine 2nd and 3rd Trimesters: ASMQ FDC or DHA-Pip		Pf: Quinine (30 mg/kg /day, 7 days); Pv: CQ (25 mg/kg/day, 3 days) For 2nd and 3rd Trimesters: AL (3 days)		
Number of antimalarial drug resistance monitoring sites (total since 2008)	11	11	3	3	10	8
Number of insecticide resistance monitoring sites	12	4	N/A	10	2	>10

AL- artemether-lumefantrine; A- artesunate; M- mefloquine; FDC – Fixed-Dose Combination; DHA-dihydroartemisinin; Pip- piperaquine; CQ- chloroquine; PQ- primaquine; AQ- amodiaquine; AP- Atovaquone-proguanil; SP- sulfadoxine-pyrimethamine

The malaria situation across the GMS is very heterogeneous and ranges from countries on track for malaria elimination to countries still scaling up malaria control activities. Unlike most sub-Saharan African countries, *P. vivax* is a major cause of malaria in GMS countries and more prevalent than *P. falciparum* in some countries. Furthermore, at least 10 species of anopheline mosquitoes are involved in malaria transmission in the GMS. Primary vectors include *An. dirus*, *An. minimus* and/or *An. maculatus*. Some of these vector species are not endophilic (indoor biters). The vector mix varies with both location and season. Malaria burden is greatest in the border areas and in forest or forest-fringe areas, where the region's most efficient vector, *An. dirus*, exists. Approximately three-quarters of the reported cases in the GMS occur in Burma. The annual figures reported by the NMCPs to the World Health Organization (WHO) for the sub-region under-estimate the true burden of malaria as these only capture data from the public sector (Table 2).

Table 2. Malaria burden in the GMS from the public sector (2011-2013)

	Estimated population in malaria-endemic (high + low-risk) areas (millions)	Number of confirmed cases (by year)	Proportion due to *falciparum* (2013) (%)	Number of inpatient malaria deaths (2013)	Artemisinin resistance (suspected and confirmed)
Burma	32.0*	567,452 (2011) 480,586 (2012) **333,871 (2013)**	66.7	236	Confirmed (Tanintharyi, Kayin, Kayah, and Bago)
Cambodia	8.0	57,423 (2011) 40,476 (2012) **21,309 (2013)**	33.3	12	Confirmed (Battambang, Oddar Meanchey, Pailin, Pursat, Preah Vihear)
China	579.5	3,367 (2011) 2,603 (2012) **4,086 (2013)**	71.1	23	Suspected (Yunnan)
Lao PDR	4.0	17,835 (2011) 46,202 (2012) **38,131 (2013)**	64.4	28	Confirmed in Champasack and Attapeu (2013)
Thailand	33.5	24,897 (2011) 32,569 (2012) **33,302 (2013)**	43.4	37	Confirmed (Kanchanaburi, Ranong, Tak, Ubon Ratchatani)
Viet Nam	34.4	16,612 (2011) 19,638 (2012) **17,128 (2013)**	55.7	6	Confirmed in Binh Phuoc (2009), Gia Lai (2010), Dak Nong and Quang Nam (2012)

Source: World Malaria Report, 2014
* This estimate reported in the World Malaria Report is based on population figures prior to the 2014 National Census. The current estimate of the population at risk is approximately 26.8 million.

Over the past decade, GMS countries have made tremendous progress in reducing the number of malaria cases and deaths reported through the public sector. From 1998 to 2010, the six countries have collectively reported an 81% reduction in the annual number of deaths attributed to malaria. Multiple factors have contributed to this reduction. Governments and partners have made malaria control a priority by increasing investments, successfully garnering international funding, strengthening political will, integrating malaria control efforts into national health systems, expanding access to basic malaria services, and improving cross-border collaboration. It is also likely that other factors such as environmental changes, deforestation, economic development, urbanization, demographic stabilization, greater political stability, and improved coverage of basic health services have impacted malaria morbidity and mortality in the GMS. Despite this progress, pockets of malaria transmission remain particularly in forested areas and along international borders.

3. *Strategic updates in the GMS*

Malaria elimination in the GMS: In November 2014, regional leaders of 14 Asia-Pacific countries and those from the United States, China, Japan, and Australia, made an unprecedented commitment at the 9th East Asia Summit (EAS) to eliminate malaria across the region by 2030. This renewed attention and goal of elimination comes at an important juncture to address artemisinin resistance by eliminating malaria altogether in the region. Co-chaired by the Australian and Vietnamese Prime Ministers, the Asia-Pacific Leaders Malaria Alliance (APLMA) have been tasked to develop a roadmap to achieve malaria elimination in the region, to be presented to the 10th EAS in Malaysia in 2015. Furthermore, WHO's Strategy for Malaria Elimination in the GMS (2015–2030) and the WHO Global Technical Strategy for malaria (2016–2030) are aligned with this regional goal of malaria elimination.

Artemisinin resistance: More recent evidence from the mostly PMI-supported drug efficacy network of therapeutic efficacy studies (TES) and other research groups suggests that artemisinin resistance is more widespread than previously thought. On January 2014, the WHO expanded its definition of Tier 1 artemisinin resistance areas to include Champasack Province in southern Lao PDR, western Cambodia, as well as reclassified Bago East, Kayin, and Kayah states in Burma as Tier 1 areas (formerly categorized as Tier 2). Furthermore, molecular investigations characterizing the degree of genetic relatedness of different artemisinin-resistant strains suggests that the overarching geographic distribution of artemisinin resistance in the Mekong likely arises out of a combination of local emergence *and* geographic spread.

4. *Integration, collaboration, and coordination*

Funding

The tremendous progress made in the region to date has paralleled the increase in malaria funding from external sources in recent years. As a whole, the region has been very successful in obtaining support from the Global Fund. All six countries have had at least one Global Fund grant; totaling over $500 million for the GMS as a whole. However, recent allocations to Thailand and Cambodia through the New Funding Model will not maintain the same levels of support as prior grants. Table 3 details the various available funding sources, including domestic resources, for regional activities. This table includes current and active funding, and does not include potential future funding.

It is important to note that the funding landscape for the post-2016 period looks uncertain. Many of the Global Fund grants in the GMS as well as other donors such as the 3MDG in Burma will terminate by the end of 2016. It is unclear whether eligibility for and resources from Global Fund will be available to many countries in the GMS, particularly in the light of the high level political commitment for malaria elimination in the region.

Other funding sources in the region, including DFAT, the Bill and Melinda Gates Foundation (BMGF), the Asian Development Bank (ADB), and bilateral aid from countries such as Japan and South Korea, may not be adequate to maintain and expand the intensified malaria control and prevention activities needed to move towards malaria elimination.

Table 3. Current funding landscape for regional activities

Funding	Total Budget in USD (Funds Disbursed)	Duration	Key Implementing Partners	Key Activities
DFAT	5,000,000	2013-2015	WHO	WHO regional Emergency Response to Artemisinin Resistance (ERAR) hub
BMGF	10,000,000			
Global Fund RAI (ICC)	15,000,000	2014-2016	SMRU, MAM, CPI	Cross-border; inter-country coordination; Mass drug administration pilots
BMGF	29,000,000	NA	CHAI	Malaria elimination efforts in Southern Africa and the GMS
DFAT	10,000,000-12,000,000 (AUD)[1]	2015-2021	TGA	Strengthening regulatory capacity of National Medicine Regulatory Authorities (NMRAs) in the Mekong
DFAT	16,300,000	2014 - 2017	ADB (Secretariat)	Regional Malaria and Other Communicable Disease Threats Trust Fund
DFID	19,400,000			

Sources: World Malaria Report 2014; www.theglobalfund.org; www.gatesfoundation.org; www.3df.org; www.3mdg.org; www.adb.org

DFAT: Department of Foreign Affairs and Trade; DFID: Department for International Development; RAI: Regional Artemisinin Resistance; ICC: Inter-Country Component; SMRU: Shoklo-Mahidol Research Unit; MAM: Medical Action Myanmar (Burma); CPI: Community Partners International; CHAI: Clinton Health Access Initiative; TGA: Therapeutic Goods Administration; ADB: Asian Development Bank

Regional Initiatives

Emergency Response to Artemisinin Resistance (2013-2015)

Following the Joint Assessment of the Response to Artemisinin Resistance in the GMS in 2011 supported by international development partners, WHO's Emergency Response to Artemisinin Resistance (ERAR) framework was developed. Funded by DFAT ($5 million) and the BMGF ($10 million), the ERAR Framework under the stewardship of WHO established a regional hub in Phnom Penh to coordinate and manage its activities.

---

[1] This level of funding is TBD

This regional framework highlights key action areas in which progress is urgently needed to address artemisinin resistance and to move towards elimination of malaria in the GMS. The overarching goal of the framework is to protect ACTs as an effective treatment for *P. falciparum* malaria. The framework seeks to do this by advocating for stakeholders to urgently scale-up and tailor interventions to address artemisinin resistance.

The ERAR framework draws attention to four priority action areas and urges partners to work in a coordinated manner to achieve: 1) Full coverage with high-quality interventions in priority areas; 2) Tighter coordination and management of field operations; 3) Better information for artemisinin resistance containment; and 4) Regional oversight and support. The ERAR Regional Hub oversees activities in Burma, Cambodia, Thailand, Lao PDR, and Viet Nam (the only country with funding for field activities), with a focus on increasing access to mobile and migrant populations and operational research.

Regional Artemisinin Initiative (RAI) (2014-2016)

In support of the ERAR Framework to respond in a coordinated manner to artemisinin resistance, the Global Fund's RAI was developed to support the implementation of this framework. This grant of $100 million over three years to the five countries in the GMS includes $15 million for a regional inter-country component. Funds are channeled through a regional Principal Recipient (UNOPS) to sub-recipients at country level. Oversight of the inter-country component is coordinated by the Regional Steering Committee, which has prioritized cross-border activities to reach migrant and mobile populations, including surveillance, mapping, information-sharing, and cross-border communication and collaboration. Furthermore, screening and presumptive treatment approaches (including targeted malaria elimination (TME)) is being evaluated initially in difficult-to-reach areas along the Thai-Burma border and will be expanded to other areas if shown to be effective.

The objectives of the RAI include:

1. Trans-border activities, reaching migrants and mobile populations, including surveillance, mapping and information, communication and information-sharing, diagnosis, treatment and follow-up, strengthening cross border communication and collaboration.
2. Monitoring impact, including cross-sectional point prevalence surveys in areas of focused interventions.
3. Integration of data sets from country data systems (in collaboration with the ERAR Hub).
4. Independent monitoring and evaluation.
5. ACT efficacy studies in areas with failing efficacy of first-line treatments, supplementing or adding to the WHO-coordinated TES. (See footnote for funding sources[1]).
6. Eliminating oral artemisinin monotherapy in the private sector.

---

[1] USAID and PMI have funded the majority of TES in the GMS since 2000 and 2011, respectively

7. Setting up a collection system for filter paper blood spots for resistance tracking. (This activity will be funded from sources other than the RAI).

Asia Pacific Leaders Malaria Alliance (APLMA)

Established at the 2013 East Asia Summit, the Asia Pacific Leaders Malaria Alliance (APLMA) is co-chaired by the Prime Ministers of Viet Nam and Australia. Similar to the African Leaders' Malaria Alliance (ALMA), APLMA's aim is to foster cooperation among governments and development partners for long-term response to malaria and communicable diseases in the region. With its Secretariat at the ADB, APLMA was set up as a high-level political advocacy platform to accelerate political commitment, mobilize country and regional action, and track progress in line with global targets.

Under APLMA, two taskforces have been established: 1) Access to Quality and Affordable Medicines and Other Technologies Taskforce and 2) Regional Financing for Malaria Taskforce.

Asian Development Bank Regional Malaria Trust Fund (RMTF)

In 2013, the ADB established a health financing facility which provides financing for activities designed to curb regional epidemics. This regional trust fund is envisaged as a fund for communicable diseases in the long term; however, in the short term the focus will be full support to malaria elimination and containment of artemisinin-resistant malaria with the aim of addressing urgent gaps in the response to drug-resistant malaria in South East Asia and help prevent its spread to Africa. The RMTF focuses its efforts on strengthened regional leadership; increased financing for malaria; increased availability, market share and use of quality-assured commodities; increased availability and use of quality information, tools and technology on malaria and other communicable disease threats; improved national capacity to detect and respond to drug-resistant malaria and other communicable disease threats; and addressing malaria in large commercial and development projects.

USG coordination

Lower Mekong Initiative

PMI embraces the goals of the Lower Mekong Initiative (LMI), a multinational partnership between Cambodia, Lao PDR, Burma, Thailand, Viet Nam, and the United States, established to support integrated sub-regional cooperation among the five Lower Mekong countries. The LMI serves as a platform to address complex, transnational development and policy challenges in the Lower Mekong sub-region. Specifically, PMI objectives for the LMI include: 1) focusing on malaria and the need to develop and strengthen a coordinated response; 2) prevention and control of counterfeit and substandard medications; 3) fostering regional collaboration to support implementation of the International Health Regulations and regional-level emphasis on surveillance and response; and 4) sharing good practices across USG health initiatives. Furthermore, cross-border and migrant issues are concerns for LMI. Burma joined the initiative in 2012, ensuring a strong geographic overlap between the PMI GMS countries and the LMI. Along with the United States, Burma is the co-chair of the Agriculture and Food Security Pillar to improve agriculture and food security sector growth throughout the Mekong sub-region in an environmentally sustainable manner.

Other USG partners

The Department of Defense's Armed Forces Research Institute of Medical Sciences (AFRIMS) has been conducting clinical research and surveillance activities in western Cambodia since 2003. After AFRIMS conducted the first study to document artemisinin resistance in 2008, subsequent research has focused on determining optimal dosing strategies for the artemisinin component of ACTs, and assessing treatment responses to first-line ACTs in Thailand and Cambodia. Currently AFRIMS is partnering with Cambodia's National Centre for Parasitology, Entomology, and Malaria (CNM) and the Royal Cambodian Armed Forces to build malaria capacity in the military sector. AFRIMS' work has been pivotal in informing national treatment policies being developed by CNM.

The Department of Defense's Naval Malaria Research Center-Asia also conducts drug resistance and clinical efficacy monitoring in the Mekong Region, focusing much of its activity in Viet Nam. Current activities include evaluating the efficacy of artemether-lumefantrine and characterizing malaria epidemiology with different levels of endemicity to allow more effective application of limited resources.

The Department of Health and Human Services, National Institutes of Health (NIH), through the National Institute of Allergy and Infectious Diseases, conducts basic research in Cambodia to improve knowledge of malaria pathogenesis and protection to aid in the development of new antimalarial therapeutics and vaccines. NIH has studied parasite clearance rates in response to artemisinin in 500 patients from western, northern, and eastern Cambodia and, by studying clinical responses to dihydroartemisinin-piperaquine (DHA-Pip) in the northern provinces, directly impacting national treatment guidelines.

Since 2011, PMI has partnered with Peace Corps to expand malaria prevention activities throughout Africa and provide Peace Corps Volunteers (PCVs) with the best resources on malaria prevention. In Asia, a total of 182 PCVs currently work in Cambodia (health and education sectors) and Thailand (youth development and education). In Burma, Peace Corps is setting up a program and placement of new PCVs is planned in 2016. PMI/Burma and PMI/Cambodia will look at the possibility of partnering with Peace Corps in the future.

5. *PMI goal, objectives, strategic areas, and key indicators*

Under the PMI Strategy for 2015-2020, the U.S. Government's goal is to work with PMI-supported countries and partners to further reduce malaria deaths and substantially decrease malaria morbidity, towards the long-term goal of elimination. Building upon the progress to date in PMI-supported countries, PMI will work with NMCPs and partners to accomplish the following objectives by 2020:

1. Reduce malaria mortality by one-third from 2015 levels in PMI-supported countries, achieving a greater than 80% reduction from PMI's original 2000 baseline levels.

2. Reduce malaria morbidity in PMI-supported countries by 40% from 2015 levels.

3. Assist at least five PMI-supported countries to meet the World Health Organization's (WHO) criteria for national or sub-national pre-elimination.[1]

These objectives will be accomplished by emphasizing five core areas of strategic focus:
- Achieving and sustaining scale of proven interventions
- Adapting to changing epidemiology and incorporating new tools
- Improving countries' capacity to collect and use information
- Mitigating risk against the current malaria control gains
- Building capacity and health systems towards full country ownership

To track progress toward achieving and sustaining scale of proven interventions (area of strategic focus #1), PMI will continue to track the key indicators recommended by the Roll Back Malaria Monitoring and Evaluation Reference Group (RBM MERG) as listed below:

- Proportion of households with at least one insecticide-treated net (ITN)
- Proportion of households with at least one ITN for every two people
- Proportion of children under five years old who slept under an ITN the previous night
- Proportion of pregnant women who slept under an ITN the previous night
- Proportion of children under five years old with fever in the last two weeks for whom advice or treatment was sought
- Proportion of children under five with fever in the last two weeks who had a finger or heel stick
- Proportion receiving an ACT among children under five years old with fever in the last two weeks who received any antimalarial drugs

At a regional level, PMI GMS activities will support efforts to conduct TES to monitor artemisinin resistance in all six countries and with particular intensity in areas where there is evidence of confirmed or potential emergence of artemisinin resistance. PMI will lead this effort and ensure technical capacity and timely reporting with engagement of national governments to take ownership of these efforts and encourage cost-sharing as other interested donors provide resources for expansion. PMI will also support efforts to strengthen national drug regulatory bodies, ensure that critical bottlenecks in the supply chain system are removed to ensure availability of the most effective antimalarials, address impediments to the availability of effective commodities, and combat use of sub-standard and counterfeit drugs that contribute to increased drug resistance.

6. *Progress on coverage/impact indicators to date in the GMS*

---

[1] http://whqlibdoc.who.int/publications/2007/9789241596084_eng.pdf

Although some of the standard indicators adopted in the GMS differ from those in Africa, several indicators, mostly measuring ITN ownership and use, remain applicable to this sub-region. Table 4 shows the most recent figures for the standard indicators being used by PMI, where survey data are available:

Table 4. National and sub-national survey data for the GMS countries

Indicator	Burma MARC (2011-2012)	Cambodia CMS (2007)	Cambodia CMS (2010)	Cambodia CMS (2013)	Cambodia Migrants Zone 1, (2010-2011)	Thailand Migrant RDS, Ranong (2012)	Thailand TMS (2012)	Laos Lao PDR (LSIS, 2012)	Viet Nam MICS (2006)	Viet Nam MICS (2011)
Malaria prevalence (%)	0.5	2.6	0.9	0.1 (slide) 1.5 (PCR)	-	0	0.1 (PCR)	-	-	-
Households with at least one net (%)	97.4	100	99.4	99.7	-	83-94	92.2	94	99	95.5
Households with at least one ITN (%)	35.1	42.6	74.7	89.5	25-53	-	46.5	50	19	9.5
Persons who slept under an ITN the previous night (%)	15.9	25.3	52.6	59.9	6-27	1-2	28.7	-	-	-
Children under five years old who slept under an ITN the previous night (%)	19.4	28.0	56.3	63.3	-	-	32.5	43.2	5	9.4
Pregnant women who slept under an ITN the previous night (%)	20.3	28.1	59.1	61.5	-	-	36.2	43.2	-	11.3

MARC: Myanmar (Burma) Artemisinin Resistance Containment Project; CMS: Cambodia Malaria Survey; TMS: Thailand Malaria Survey; ITN: insecticide-treated net; MICS: Multiple Indicator Cluster Survey; RDS: Respondent-driven sampling; LSIS: Lao Social Indicator Survey

Most of the GMS countries have relied primarily on routine health management information system (HMIS) data for planning and monitoring their malaria activities, but continue to use nationally-representative cross-sectional surveys such as the DHS, MIS, and MICS to measure outcome and impact. The exception has been Cambodia, which has conducted national malaria surveys in 2004, 2007, 2010, and 2013 as well as a Demographic and Health Survey (DHS) in 2010 per their national M&E plan. Burma conducted a survey in containment zones 1 and 2 that sampled households, health facilities, and drug outlets in late 2011 as part of the Myanmar (Burma) Artemisinin Resistance Containment (MARC) Project. The surveys conducted to date for Thailand, Cambodia, and Burma are described in more detail in their individual country sections.

In general, large-scale surveys have been used to obtain ITN ownership and use data e.g. in Lao PDR's Social Indicator Survey in 2012 and Viet Nam's Multiple Indicator Cluster Survey in 2011. Although Thailand has a robust malaria surveillance system, biomarkers were included in the 2012 malaria survey to assess the usefulness of polymerase chain reaction (PCR) and serology. The Thailand and MARC surveys were largely designed and harmonized with the Cambodian surveys. Overall, these surveys from the sub-region show high levels of conventional bed net ownership with low levels of ITN ownership and use. Malaria prevalence estimates from Cambodia, Thailand, and Burma show very low levels at <1%; however, Burma was sampled after the peak transmission season. Migrant surveys using a respondent-driven sampling methodology to generate a representative estimate show lower levels of ITN ownership and use compared to the resident populations both in Cambodia at the Thai border and in Thailand at the southern Burmese border. Lao PDR completed a DHS with a malaria module in 2011-12 showing relatively high ITN coverage, but lower use of appropriate diagnostics and treatment.

Malaria surveillance systems vary greatly amongst the GMS countries. Thailand's surveillance system is probably most comprehensive; whereas the systems in countries such as Burma and Lao PDR are nascent and will require further strengthening. Much of the malaria data from the HMIS and malaria information systems currently remain focused on morbidity and mortality (Table 2). In addition, the HMIS would probably not be able to capture LLIN coverage and use as well as care-seeking indicators relevant for the malaria program. Implementing some targeted household surveys to capture these monitoring indicators may still be useful and needed to complement the routine data. A Malaria Indicator Survey (MIS) is planned for Burma in late 2015 to improve our understanding of the burden of malaria and coverage of interventions in the country. Lao PDR is currently planning to conduct a follow-on national Social Indicator Survey in 2016 to provide estimates to monitor nutritional status, reproductive health needs, and prevention of infectious diseases including malaria.

At the same time, as malaria incidence declines and malaria becomes more heterogeneous, the need for large-scale population-based surveys will wane and more emphasis will be placed on strengthening routine surveillance systems. Countries such as Thailand and even Cambodia will need to rely more and more on improving their surveillance systems as malaria continues to decline. Furthermore, most routine surveillance systems in the region are not comprehensive and currently are limited to the public sector only. Data from the private sector is grossly under-estimated in the region and further work is needed to improve this.

III. THAILAND and REGIONAL

(A) Strategy

1. Introduction

Initially with USAID/RDMA and then PMI funding in 2011, the USG has led efforts in the fight against drug-resistant malaria in the GMS. Through scale up and increasing coverage and use of proven effective interventions, PMI's strategy aims to drive the burden of malaria down towards malaria elimination. Although Burma and Cambodia Missions now receive direct funding for malaria, regional programming continues to play a critical role in supporting and coordinating activities across the region. In support of the bilateral Missions, the role of USAID/RDMA focuses on three key areas: 1) connecting GMS countries and Missions; 2) providing technical assistance through a regional service-centered approach; and 3) designing, procuring, and/or managing projects for non-presence and/or non-bilateral countries.

The PMI/RDMA team provides technical oversight over regionally managed projects such as the multi-country TES network for antimalarial drug resistance surveillance through WHO, support for regional capacity building and training through the **Asian Collaborative Training Network for Malaria** (ACTMalaria), and strengthening national drug authorities to detect and remove substandard or counterfeit malaria medicines. Furthermore, to allow for flexibility in addressing malaria outbreaks and unforeseen gaps in the region, direct support for some malaria control activities in non-presence countries through the regional platform has its advantages, as demonstrated by PMI's recent support in Lao PDR to respond to a malaria outbreak.

Despite the expansion of PMI's bilateral programs in Burma and Cambodia, specialized malaria technical expertise remains available through the RDMA regional platform. The complex technical challenges confronted by NMCPs across the region require a solid understanding of the unique programmatic issues and regional context. The RDMA regional platform has technical expertise ready to assist NMCPs and partners, including those in non-presence countries, as needed, to help to address cross-cutting, trans-boundary issues that affect all GMS countries. As NMCPs transition from malaria control to elimination, there will be highly technical topics that will require support e.g. vector control with outdoor transmission and mobile populations, case management of *P. falciparum* in the setting of artemisinin resistance and *P. vivax* in the setting of severe glucose-6-phosphate dehydrogenase (G6PD) deficient variants, surveillance and M&E in low transmission and now elimination settings, and implementation and evaluation of elimination-specific activities (e.g. reactive case detection). In addition, capacity-building at the regional level for NMCPs to address adequately complex technical as well as programmatic challenges remains a critical need. Building capacity in the region is not only consistent with PMI's new strategy, but a necessity as programs scale-up and transition to elimination.

Outlined in the new PMI Strategy (2015-2020), USG funds support working with national malaria programs and partners to further reduce malaria deaths and substantially decrease malaria morbidity towards the long-term goal of elimination. The PMI/Mekong team provides technical support to Thailand and Lao PDR as the countries develop their plans towards achieving malaria elimination and sub-national elimination by 2024 and 2030, respectively. In particular, the PMI/Mekong team works to increase capacity for use of strategic information and strengthen national malaria surveillance and M&E systems for malaria control and elimination.

This FY 2016 Malaria Operational Plan (MOP) presents the implementation plan for PMI/Mekong, based on the strategies of PMI and relevant National Malaria Control Programs (NMCP). Developed in consultation with the NMCP and partners, activities described in the MOP support the national malaria control strategic plans and build on investments made by PMI and other partners including the Global Fund to improve and expand malaria-related services. This document briefly reviews the current status of malaria control policies and interventions for Thailand and the GMS, describes progress to date, identifies challenges and unmet needs to achieving the targets of the NMCP and PMI, and provides a description of activities that are planned with FY 2016 funding.

2. Malaria situation in Thailand/GMS

Thailand

Malaria cases mainly occur in provinces bordering Burma and Cambodia. The groups at risk for malaria in Thailand consist of refugees in camps, workers in rubber plantations and fruit orchards, people who spend the night in the forest (including the military), and ethnic minority groups living along Thai-Burma border. Introduction of rubber plantations in many parts of the country during the past ten years and movement of workers has resulted in emergence of sporadic new foci. Due to labor shortages, Thailand has been drawing large numbers of migrant workers from Burma and Cambodia. Large numbers of migrant workers live and work along border districts and provinces where malaria is still endemic while others move back and forth between home communities and various work destinations in Thailand. The situation poses a risk for transporting malaria from place to place. Though national malaria incidence is decreasing, recent demand for expensive hard wood has precipitated illegal logging in the forests in the northeastern province adjacent to southern Lao PDR and north of Cambodia, leading to recent spikes in malaria cases in the area.

The graph below shows malaria cases among indigenous Thais and migrants residing in Thailand for six months or longer (M1) together, while cases among migrants living less than six months are referred to as M2. In 2014, the total number of malaria cases was 45,600, down from 55,226 cases the previous year. The Annual Parasite Index (API) was 0.49 per 1,000 population, and *P. falciparum* accounted for 41% of the malaria cases reported. These cases included those who crossed the border and sought treatment at malaria posts and health facilities in Thailand.

Compared to the other countries in the GMS, Thailand's malaria surveillance data is the most comprehensive which allows the NMCP to update village-level malaria risk on an annual basis. In 2014, the NMCP determined that local malaria transmission was still occurring in 46 out of 77 provinces; 155 out of 930 districts; and 5,502 out of 74,956 villages.

Figure 2: Trend of malaria morbidity and mortality in Thailand among Thais, M1, M2, and refugees (2009-2014) (Source: BVBD)

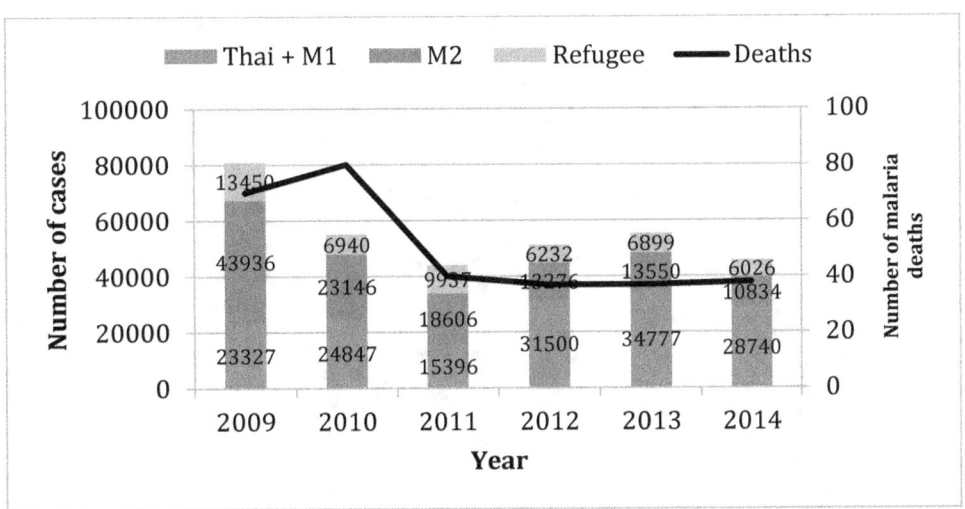

The NMCP stratifies malaria transmission risk for each village according to the following criteria:

- A1: perennial transmission area (transmission reported for at least six months per year)
- A2: periodic transmission area (transmission reported for less than six months per year)
- B1: high and moderate receptivity (transmission not reported within the last three years but primary and secondary vectors present)
- B2: low and no receptivity (transmission not reported within the last three years and primary and secondary vectors absent, suspected vector may be present)

Using such malaria risk stratification, BVBD is able to identify indigenous transmission (A1 + A2) as illustrated in Figure 3. Despite the decrease in malaria cases between 2013 and 2014, surveillance data suggests that malaria transmission is occurring in villages which previously did not have transmission particularly along the international borders with Lao PDR, Cambodia, and Burma. The increase in the number of villages in Thailand with malaria transmission is largely due to the malaria outbreak in Lao PDR which started in Attapeu (late 2011) and has spread to four other southern provinces, most notably Champasack. Champasack Province borders Thailand and these border provinces have detected increases in malaria cases in 2013 and 2014 on both sides of the Lao-Thailand border.

Figure 3: Map of villages with malaria transmission in Thailand, 2013 (left) vs. 2014 (right) (Source: BVBD)

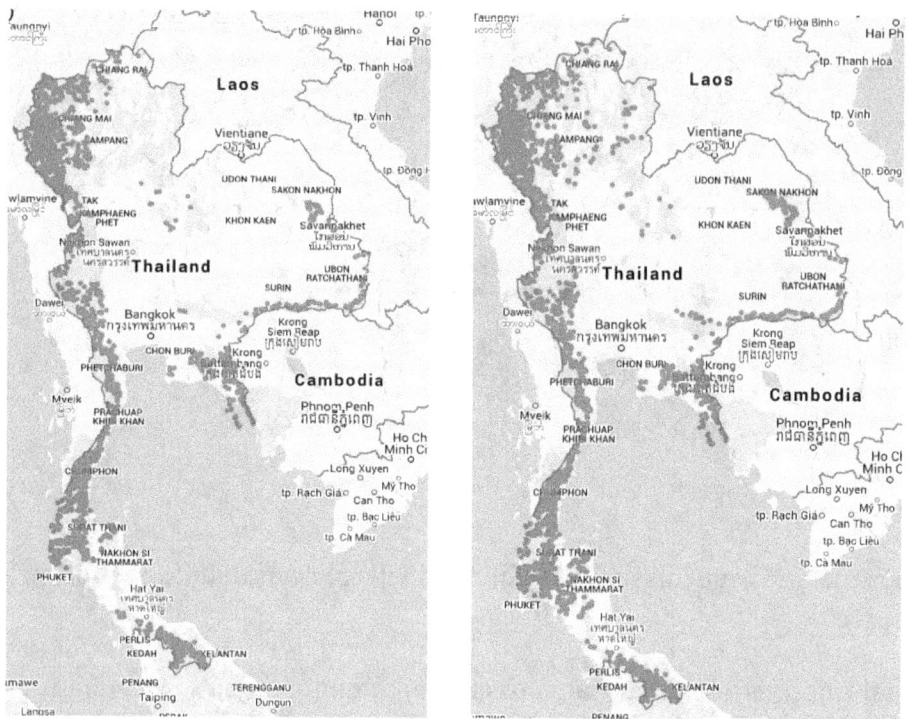

Note: Light green color represents forested areas and red dots indicate villages with malaria transmission

Lao PDR

The intensity of malaria transmission varies between different ecological zones: from very low transmission in the plains along the Mekong River and in areas of high altitude, to intense transmission (API>30) in remote, forested areas of the south. *Plasmodium falciparum* has been the predominant species, accounting for 95% of all recorded malaria cases, although recent surveys suggest a *P. vivax* prevalence rate of 33% and upwards of 63% in the northern provinces. Groups at greatest risk include ethnic minorities, forest and agricultural workers, miners, and children below the age of five years.

Figure 4: Stratification of villages by malaria incidence in Lao PDR (2006-2008) (Source: CMPE)

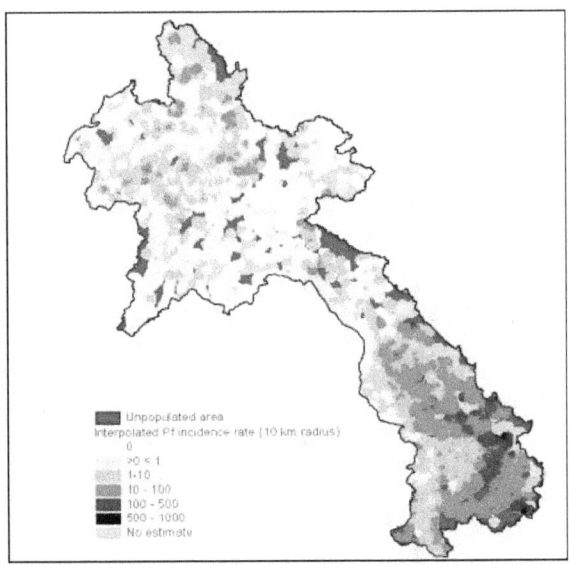

Significant reductions in malaria transmission have been reported since the large-scale introduction of ACTs and ITNs, in conjunction with socioeconomic and environmental changes due to deforestation. The annual number of uncomplicated malaria cases (probable and confirmed) fell from 40,106 in 2000 to 20,800 cases in 2010 and the number of malaria deaths in hospitals dropped from 350 in 2000 to 24 in 2010; however, the recent influx of seasonal workers of mainly Vietnamese origin has led to alarming increases of reported malaria cases in the southern provinces bordering Cambodia and Viet Nam resulting in the increase in API since 2011 (Figure 5).

Beginning in 2011, the Centre for Malaria, Parasitology, and Entomology (CMPE) began utilizing a more targeted approach to the distribution of malaria control measures. As detailed in their 2011-2015 National Strategy for Malaria Control and Pre-Elimination, rather than providing ITNs, RDTs, and ACTs in all villages, these resources were to be reserved for the villages with the highest burden of malaria. A survey of all malaria cases reported between 2006-2008 in each village was performed in 2009, and villages were stratified based on malaria incidence into four groups: Stratum 1 (0-0.1 cases/1,000 persons), Stratum 2 (0.1-10 cases/1,000 persons), Stratum 3 (>10 cases/1,000 persons) and Unknown (insufficient data). About two-thirds of the villages were determined to fall into Stratum 1, and the rest were divided between the remaining strata. Most of the low-strata villages were in the north, whereas high-strata villages tended to be concentrated in the south. Approximately 95% of all reported malaria cases are from five provinces in southern Lao PDR (Saravane, Savannakhet, Champasack, Sekong, and Attapeu).

Figure 5: Trend of malaria morbidity and mortality in Lao PDR (2000-2014) (Source: CMPE)

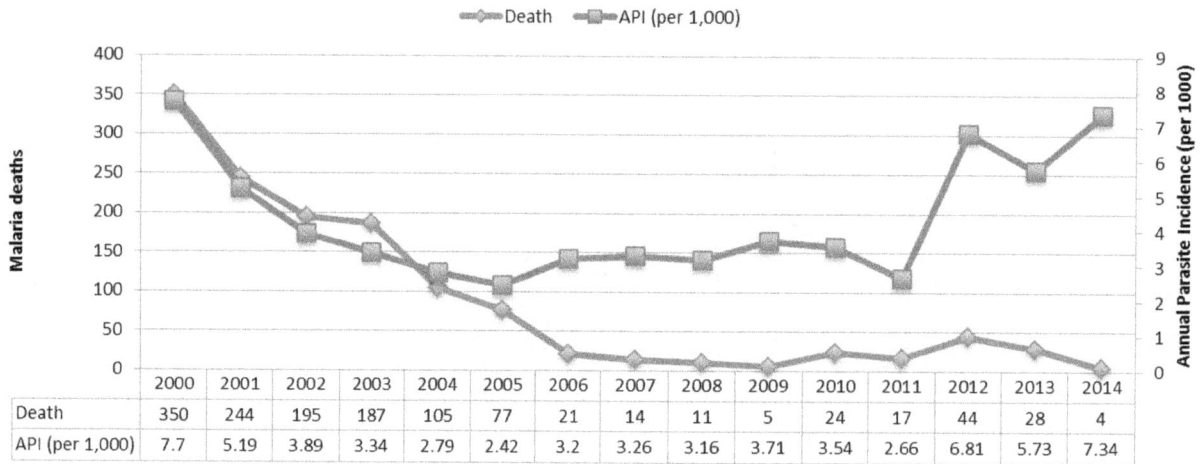

	2000	2001	2002	2003	2004	2005	2006	2007	2008	2009	2010	2011	2012	2013	2014
Death	350	244	195	187	105	77	21	14	11	5	24	17	44	28	4
API (per 1,000)	7.7	5.19	3.89	3.34	2.79	2.42	3.2	3.26	3.16	3.71	3.54	2.66	6.81	5.73	7.34

Viet Nam

In Viet Nam, malaria occurs in remote forest and forest fringe communities, which are often inhabited by marginalized groups, including ethnic minorities and migrant settlers. The distribution of ITNs has occurred in all endemic villages with coverage estimated to be 70% by the NMCP. Viet Nam, like other countries in the GMS, has a longstanding culture of bed net use that precedes the introduction of ITNs. As a component of Viet Nam's national malaria control strategy, the program treats approximately 4 to 5 million existing bed nets each year with insecticide. In recent years, through Global Fund support, Viet Nam has introduced LLINs for certain provinces of the country, especially for hard-to-reach areas. In addition to this, the NMCP uses indoor residual spraying (IRS) to cover an additional 2 million people residing in hyper-endemic areas, where ITN use is low. The burden is concentrated at the border areas of Cambodia and Lao PDR (Figure 6). Viet Nam has reduced malaria cases from 293,016 to 27,868 and deaths from 148 to 6, between 2000 and 2014, respectively.

Figure 6: Malaria risk stratification in Viet Nam, 2009 (Source: NIMPE)

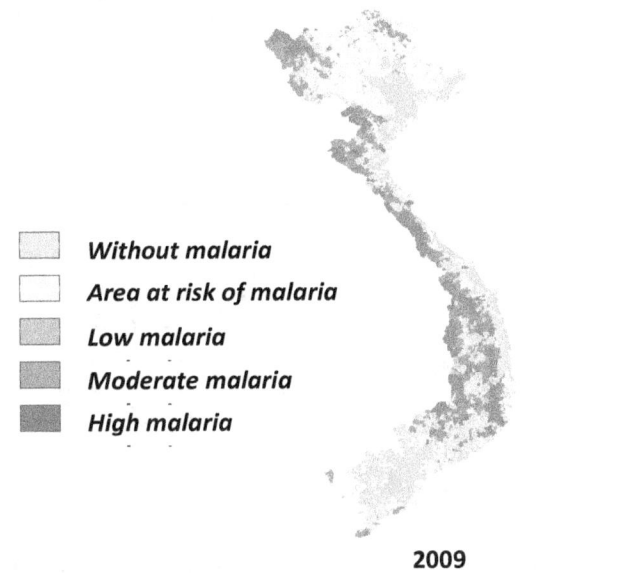

- Without malaria
- Area at risk of malaria
- Low malaria
- Moderate malaria
- High malaria

2009

China

The People's Republic of China is mainly affected by *P. vivax; P. falciparum* is endemic in only two provinces, Yunnan and Hainan. Because Yunnan Province shares borders with Burma, Laos, and Viet Nam, it is the province in China of greatest concern for malaria and, as such, is included in regional GMS malaria control strategies. The Bureau of Disease Control located within the Ministry of Health (MOH) is responsible for managing malaria control activities while the Provincial Health and County Health Bureaus manage the provincial- and county-level efforts. The new 2010–2020 National Malaria Strategy aims to eliminate malaria from all provinces by 2020 with an intermediate goal of elimination from all areas except the borders of Yunnan Province by 2015.[1] In China, counties are classified by type I-IV (Figure 7). In Yunnan, Type I counties are concentrated along the Burma border where malaria is particularly problematic among people crossing the border and ethnic minority groups. Although China has demonstrated a decline in malaria morbidity and mortality, control efforts are hampered by the continuous influx of migrants from Burma.

---

[1] From Malaria Control to Elimination: A Revised National Malaria Strategy 2010-2015. The People's Republic of China.

Figure 7: Malaria risk stratification in China by county (Source: MOH)

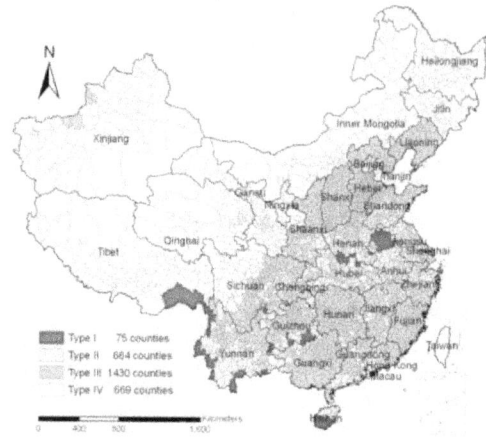

- Type I represents the counties in China with confirmed local case(s) in the last 3 years, with at least one year having an annual incidence >=1/10,000
- Type II represents counties with confirmed local case(s) in the last 3 years, annual incidence <1/10,000.
- Type III represents counties with no local case for at least 3 years, only imported cases.
- Type IV represents counties with no history of any locally transmitted cases, only imported cases.

The Chinese treatment policy calls for use of ACTs, primarily DHA-Pip. The strategy for vector control is based on epidemiologic stratification. In the high-risk areas with vector presence, the program aims to achieve 100% LLIN coverage and uses IRS in focal transmission areas. Additionally, the program designs specific interventions for special populations such as forest workers and migrant populations.

Beyond technical support for the therapeutic efficacy monitoring network, PMI does not provide direct implementation support in Viet Nam or in China at this time. The subsequent sections of the Thailand/Regional MOP will focus on Thailand and Lao PDR. However, the importance of continued engagement with Viet Nam and China is recognized, particularly on drug resistance, drug quality monitoring, and more recently, on regional malaria elimination efforts.

3. Health system delivery structure and organization

Thailand

The Thai Malaria Control Program has been a vertical program from its inception in 1949 until 1996. In 1996, it was partially merged with other vector-borne disease programs (Dengue fever and Filariasis). It is now called the Bureau of Vector-borne Diseases (BVBD) within the Department of Disease Control (DDC) in the Ministry of Public Health. It is responsible for malaria-related research, generating policy for malaria control, and evaluating the program. At the regional level, the organization consists of 12 Disease Prevention and Control offices. Throughout the country, there are 39 Vector-borne Disease centers at the provincial level and 301 Vector-borne Disease units at the district level that are responsible for the prevention and control of malaria as well as other vector-borne diseases. There are currently 329 malaria clinics throughout the country. Additionally, village malaria volunteers are actively involved in prevention and control activities in each community.

Malaria services are provided both by the vertical program through BVBD's networks of malaria clinics and through general health service facilities through district and provincial hospitals. Availability of Global Fund support in the past has boosted the role of BVBD as it provides sub-grants to Provincial Health Offices to implement community-based services through malaria posts and border malaria posts making the services easily accessible to migrants. Health workers at malaria clinics use microscopes while those at malaria posts use rapid diagnostic tests (RDTs).

Currently, the NMCP is undergoing decentralization and reducing the number of specialized field malaria officials and funds.

Figure 8: Organizational structure of Thailand MOPH (Source: BVBD)

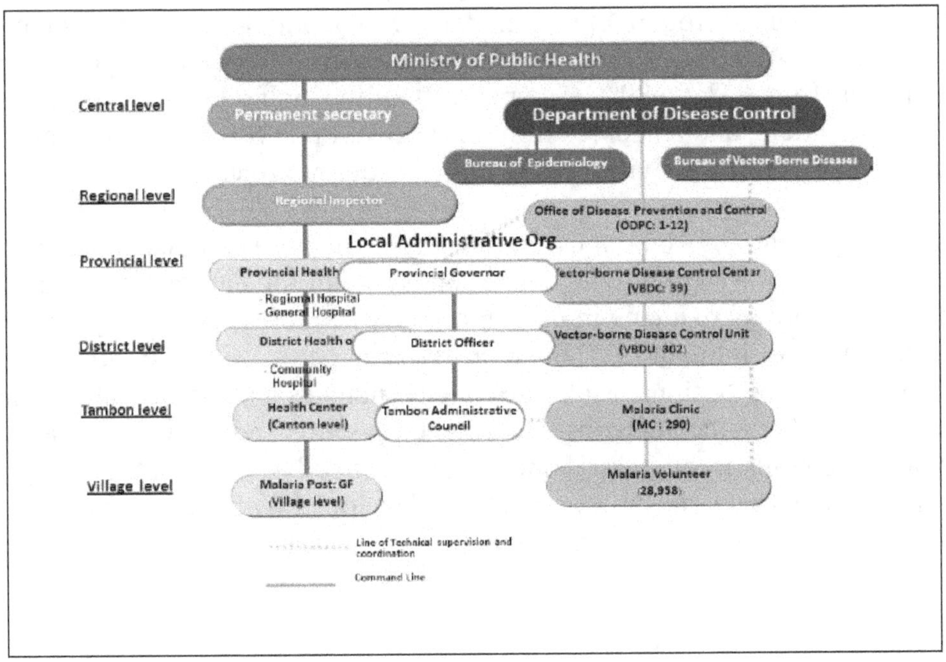

Lao PDR

The Ministry of Health has called for more integrated approaches, particularly for maternal and child health and immunization, decentralized service delivery methods, improved methods of health care financing, a unified and simplified health information system, and an emphasis on quality improvement in the next five years, rather than quantity improvement, which was emphasized over the past few years.

The public health system is predominant, although a private alternative is growing. There are around 1,865 private pharmacies and 254 private clinics, mainly in urban areas. The state system is underutilized, especially in the peripheral areas. In its efforts to increase access through village volunteers and village revolving drug funds, the Government has managed to reach 5,226 villages.

Malaria activities are centralized at CMPE which oversees 17 Provincial Anti-Malaria Stations. Under the Provincial Anti-Malaria Stations, there are 140 District Malaria Nuclei and Provincial Hospitals, including military hospitals. There are approximately 850 health centers in the country which cover nearly 2,000 malaria-endemic villages.

4. National malaria control strategy

Thailand

The goal of the current National Strategic Plan for Malaria Control and Elimination is to ensure 80% of the country will be free from locally acquired malaria transmission by the year 2016, 90% by 2018, and 95% by 2020. By 2018, the targets set for achieving this goal include: 1) reduction of API (all species) from 0.43 to 0.25 per 1,000 population; 2) reduction of malaria mortality rate from 0.07 to 0.05 per 100,000 population; and 3) increase the percent of non-transmission districts from 84% to 90%. The majority of the malaria burden in Thailand occurs along international borders; and resources from the Global Fund SSF and RAI grants target malaria control and prevention activities along these border provinces.

The National Strategic Plan for Malaria Control and Elimination is aligned with the principles of the WHO's Global Malaria Program. The overarching goal of the national malaria program is to contribute to Thai welfare by reducing malaria morbidity and mortality, by reducing the size of transmission areas and by eliminating artemisinin-resistant parasites (in collaboration with neighboring countries). The National Malaria Strategy includes a sub-national elimination strategy which aims to strengthen existing surveillance systems and active case detection, investigation, and follow-up through implementation of directly-observed therapy (DOT). As of May 2014, a new national malaria strategy has been developed with nascent plans to integrate malaria services into local primary health services.

Lao PDR

Lao PDR is in the process of updating their new National Malaria Strategic Plan (2015-2020). The National Strategic Plan (NSP) will aim to address: 1) steps toward elimination of malaria in the northern provinces (including strategies for treatment of *P. vivax*); 2) strengthened surveillance to detect and mitigate malaria outbreaks; 3) expansion of the public-private mix network of pharmacies and clinics in the south; 4) containment strategy for artemisinin resistance; 5) multi-sectoral approach for malaria programming and diversification of funding; and 6) strengthening human resources.

5. Strategic updates

Thailand

- In 2014, Thailand launched a new National Strategic Plan (NSP) for Malaria 2014–2018 that seeks to increase the number of districts without malaria transmission up to at least 90% (baseline: 83.3%), and to reduce API to less than 0.25 per 1,000 population (baseline: 0.51). The mid-term goal of the Thailand NSP is that the majority of people are not at risk of malaria infection by 2018, and Thailand is free from malaria by 2025. BVBD also plans to integrate malaria services into local primary health services. In endemic provinces a number of health promotion hospitals have been trained to provide malaria services; these hospitals previously only provided health education and referral to malaria clinics.
- In early 2015, BVBD created a Malaria Elimination Coordination Section to raise the profile of the malaria elimination agenda in Thailand. This group will develop an operational plan for malaria elimination to be presented and approved by the Permanent Secretary in July 2015.

Lao PDR

- In collaboration with the Global Fund and PMI, a WHO Malaria Program Review (MPR) was conducted in November 2013. One of the key recommendations from this review was to update the malaria risk stratification to the district level. The previous stratification at village level was found to be too difficult to manage operationally, particularly with the limited human resources in the country.
- Additionally, the MPR recommended that the country should be divided epidemiologically into a northern region (with low malaria transmission and considered for malaria elimination) and a southern region (with continuing high burden of disease requiring aggressive malaria control and outbreak response). In its revised NSP, CMPE has developed different strategies for its varied epidemiology: continued malaria control and prevention in the 47 districts with API > 1 and pre-elimination in the 88 districts with API < 1. In the latter, CMPE will aim to conduct case investigations and strengthen reporting systems and responses. CMPE is also looking to pilot the use of primaquine for *P. vivax* and further evaluate its policy for diagnosis of G6PD deficiency.

Figure 9: Malaria risk map based on annual parasite incidence (API) by district in Lao PDR (Source: CMPE)

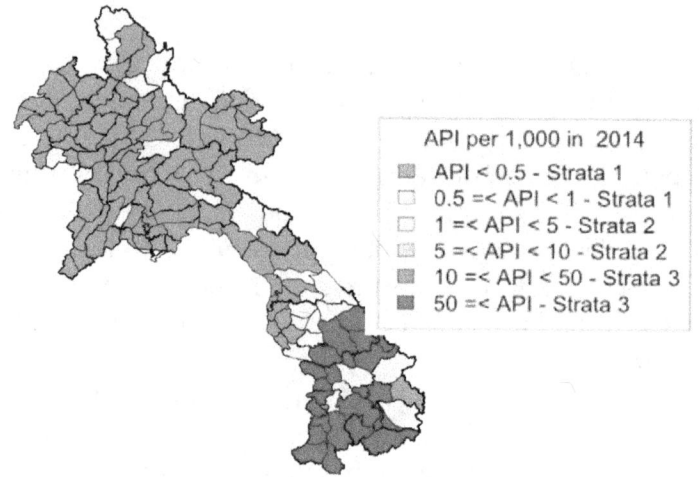

- Recent data from the TES site in Champasack indicate that 22% of patients remained positive on Day 3. Among these patients, 21/27 (78%) had Kelch13 (K13) mutations. Furthermore, preliminary data among Day 3 positive cases in Attapeu (TRAC study site conducted by the Welcome Trust) suggest two cases observed to possess the K13 mutation. With clinical TES data showing that artemisinin resistance is now present in southern Lao PDR, intensified malaria control efforts will be required to address this, particularly among these highly mobile populations along the Lao-Cambodia-Viet Nam borders.

6. Integration, collaboration, and coordination

Funding
Thailand

At present, there are two concurrent malaria projects supported by the Global Fund; these are Single Stream Funding (SSF) from Round 10 (2014-2016) and the RAI for GMS (January 2014-December 2016; 9.7 million). Together with PMI support, malaria interventions are taking place in 46 malaria-endemic provinces. The support and activities target local Thai citizens, longer-term (M1) and short-term migrants (M2), and refugees in camps and people living in conflict zones along the Thai-Burma border. The projects aim to provide 100% LLIN coverage among these populations in both A1 and A2 areas (approximately 1.8 persons per LLIN). The inter-country component of RAI will also address cross-border areas, initially between Thailand and Burma. In addition, LLINs for short-term, non-Thai residents (M2) will be provided when the person presents at a clinic with fever. Long-lasting insecticide-treated hammock nets (LLIHNs) and repellents will also be provided to special at-risk populations. In the event of a documented local focus of infection, the NMCP plans to conduct limited IRS in the areas near the index cases.

Over the period 2012 to 2015, PMI strengthened its support to Thailand and increased access to malaria prevention and treatment services among migrants and ethnic minorities residing in border provinces through the distribution of LLINs and provision of case management services from border malaria posts. This support is being phased out in 2014-2015 as some malaria posts have been transferred to the Global Fund support and some to local health authorities. PMI has been providing technical support to BVBD to ensure the quality of TES in various sentinel sites in Thailand through training in Good Clinical Practice, ethics, and clinical research implementation. Technical coordination of TES has also been provided through WHO.

Lao PDR

CMPE has in the past received funds from various donors which include the World Bank, JICA, the European Union, and the World Health Organization. Commencing in 2004, the Global Fund has been the sole source of external funding for the program which accounts for more than 90% of total program funds. With Global Fund grant management structures, there has been a gradual improvement in the financial management system with the establishment of the Principal Recipient (PR), Sub-recipients (SR) and Sub-SRs at provincial levels. The uncertainty of continued funding through the Global Fund after 2016 raises concerns about maintaining malaria control and prevention activities in Lao PDR. As a land-locked country, any resurgence of malaria in Lao PDR will inevitably affect its neighbors and jeopardize the region's goals for malaria elimination.

Table 5: Current funding landscape in Thailand, Lao PDR, Viet Nam, and China

Country	Funding	Total Budget in USD (Funds Disbursed)	Duration	Key Implementing Partners	Key Activities
Thailand	Domestic*	5,893,255			Treatment services for Thai citizens (2013 Funding)
	Global Fund SSF	29,203,469 (16,347,131)	2014-2016	BVBD, DDC (PR)	Containment of artemisinin resistance and moving towards the elimination of *Plasmodium falciparum*
	Global Fund RAI	10,000,000	2014-2016	BVBD, DDC (PR)	Artemisinin Resistance Containment
Lao PDR	Domestic*	1,122,915			Treatment services for Lao citizens
	Global Fund Transitional Funding Mechanism	7,039,151	2013 –2015	CMPE, HPA, DCDC (PR)	LLIN scale-up activities, early diagnosis and treatment, Information System, project management; private sector involvement in five southern provinces.
	Global Fund RAI	5,000,000	2014-2016	CMPE, HPA, DCDC (PR)	Artemisinin Resistance Containment
Viet Nam	Domestic*	4,523,810			Treatment services for Vietnamese citizens
	Global Fund Transitional Funding Mechanism	31,906,939 (28,711,982)	2013 - 2015	NIMPE (PR)	Community-based targeting the remaining endemic areas and mobile populations
	Global Fund Health Systems Strengthening	65,289,265 (41,862,214)	2012 - 2016	MOH (PR)	Targeting 15 project provinces plus patients suffering from HIV, TB and malaria; national pharmacovigilance system and strengthening the drug quality control network
	DFAT/BMGF	2,000,000	2013 - 2015	WHO (ERAR)	Targeting migrant populations
	Global Fund RAI	15,000,000	2014-2016	NIMPE (PR)	Artemisinin Resistance Containment
China	Domestic*	16,812,725			2013 Domestic Funding for malaria

Sources: World Malaria Report 2014; www.theglobalfund.org; www.gatesfoundation.org; www.Three Diseases Fund.org; www.adb.org; Figures in parentheses are disbursed amounts; *Funding per year

7. Progress on coverage/impact indicators to date

Thailand

Thailand had not conducted a nationwide malaria survey in several decades due to the fact that it has a fairly comprehensive routine surveillance system in place. However, with funding from the Global Fund in 2012, Thailand conducted a malariometric survey (using microscopy and PCR) to help with measuring progress and outcomes for the Global Fund grant as well as indicators for the national program. The design of the survey aimed to compare coverage of malaria interventions in at-risk villages along the Thai-Cambodia border, Thai-Burma border, and the rest of Thailand. Overall, malaria prevalence with PCR was very low (0.1%), but the survey indicated some areas for improvement in terms of coverage and use of LLINs. Approximately 80% of all people living in sampled households slept under a mosquito net the previous night; however, only 28.7% used an ITN. Household coverage and use of ITNs was slightly better in the provinces along the Thai-Cambodia border compared to the Thai-Burma border.

Lao PDR

The most recent national survey in Lao PDR was the Lao Social Indicator Survey (LSIS) conducted in 2011-2012. This survey was a household-based survey that applied the technical frameworks of the MICS and DHS, which captures data for nutrition, fertility and reproductive health, and maternal and child health, including malaria. Both the MICS (2006) and LSIS (2012) in Lao PDR indicated modest coverage of households with at least one ITN, but there were significant gaps in diagnostic testing and prompt treatment-seeking behaviors. For example, only 10% of children under five with a fever within the past two weeks were screened with a diagnostic rapid test or other method. With support from UNICEF and other partners, another follow-up LSIS is planned for 2016.

8. Challenges and opportunities

Thailand

For Thailand, one of the key challenges is addressing malaria control and prevention amongst migrant populations. Particularly as the Association of Southeast Asian Nations (ASEAN) Economic Community aims to integrate gradually the ASEAN countries starting in 2015, the flow of migrants throughout the region and into Thailand could significantly increase, and potentially contribute to the spread of artemisinin resistance as well as other infectious diseases.

Another potential threat to the progress of the malaria control and elimination program in Thailand pertains to the programmatic shift from a vertical, centrally managed program to a decentralized, integrated one. Domestic and external resources for malaria-specific activities may be threatened as the burden of the disease decreases, particularly in areas of pre-elimination and elimination.

Lao PDR

In Lao PDR, one of the major challenges is the chronic lack of human capacity and over-dependence on external resources. Issues pertaining to persistent stockouts and stock management, and poor data flow and reporting are often cited by the national malaria control program. Despite these issues, there are opportunities to make significant impact in Lao PDR with its relatively small population and established network of village volunteers. Another opportunity is the Public-Private Mix strategy that was piloted with Global Fund support in 2008 in eight districts providing commodities to private pharmacies and clinics. This approach has now been expanded to 22 districts in eight provinces. Cases detected and treated through these private pharmacies and clinics have steadily increased, and this may be an effective approach to reach populations who seek care from the private sector.

(B) Operational Plan

1. Insecticide-treated nets

NMCP/PMI objectives

All NMCPs in the GMS support free mass distribution of LLINs to targeted areas. While in the past – and to some extent now – the areas targeted were those with high levels of artemisinin resistance, NMCPs are shifting to a strategy of stratifying levels of endemicity and providing mass coverage of LLINs in areas with high malaria incidence. In areas with low endemicity, which are reorienting their programs to pre-elimination, the strategy is to ensure LLIN coverage in transmission foci; thus distribution is targeted to villages or clusters of villages with active transmission. In addition to LLINs, there is provision – sometimes at no cost and sometimes through social marketing – of LLIHNs, intended for forest workers. Traditionally, there has been a very large and active private sector sale of untreated nets of varying quality throughout the GMS. In general, household ownership of untreated nets is high, especially in rural Burma and Cambodia.

The vectors in the Mekong Region include numerous species, many of which are species complexes, but the primary vectors are *An. dirus*, *An. minimus*, and *An. maculatus*; however, vector status and relative importance is temporally and spatially heterogeneous. Malaria transmission occurs both indoors and outdoors, and LLINs will have greater or lesser impact depending upon the extent of exophily.

Much of the malaria transmission in the GMS occurs in forested and forest fringe areas, and plantations and farms where workers sleep in the open or under temporary shelters. Some reports indicate that up to 60% of infective bites occur either outdoors, or during the evening or early morning hours when people are not sleeping. The consensus of 2012 and 2013 meetings of the RBM Vector Control Working Group on outdoor malaria transmission was that LLINs/LLIHNs are effective in the GMS and wide coverage of vulnerable populations should remain a goal, with high priority given for the development and evaluation of methods to interrupt outdoor transmission. In a summary of ten publications on the efficacy of ITNs in South East Asia, eight studies reported broad effectiveness; one study reported effectiveness against one vector species but not others, and one found no measurable effectiveness against any host mosquitoes. (Efficacy of insecticide-treated nets in South East Asia: Annotated Bibliography by Anna Hoskin, Malaria Consortium report, Sept 2010). This conclusion is consistent with the early Cochrane review of Lengeler (2004) which concluded that ITNs were broadly effective across Asia.

Mosquito coils, repellents, protective clothing, and fumigation with smoke are also used within the GMS as personal protective measures. A presentation at the 2013 Vector Control Working Group meeting reported that many rubber tappers in Burma used mosquito coils attached to a hat or head lamp when tapping. There have been several efforts in Burma, Thailand, Cambodia, and Viet Nam to reinforce personal protection through use of repellents and treated materials. However, the use and effectiveness of topical repellents in different settings has not been assessed and widespread deployment has not occurred. Preliminary results of a large-scale repellent study in Cambodia showed no added protection with repellent use. There is an urgent need to identify and test new, efficacious personal protection measures for vulnerable groups.

The Thai BVBD's National Strategic Plan for Malaria Control and Elimination targets one LLIN for each resident, long-term migrant, and military personnel based in malaria-endemic villages. LLINs are to be replaced every three years. Long-lasting insecticide-treated hammock nets are distributed in endemic villages of targeted provinces where LLINs cannot be used (e.g., migrants and soldiers spending nights in the forest and on the Thai-Cambodia border). Thailand is a major net manufacturer.

The Thailand Malaria Survey conducted in 2012/2013 noted 92.2% net ownership, but only 46.5% ITN ownership with only 28.7% sleeping under an ITN the previous night. Under Thailand's Global Fund Round 10 grant, 600,000 LLINs were distributed free-of-charge in mass campaigns between October 2011 and March 2013 in 22 endemic target districts.

Progress since PMI was launched

Programs in the GMS have broadly increased coverage of LLINs and LLIHNs over the past years; the primary issue facing programs is better targeting of net distribution guided by information on malaria transmission. In Thailand, the NMCP has the needed information for effective targeting, while in other GMS countries coordination is more challenging due to dispersion of data amongst various partners.

With FY 2012 funds, 110,000 LLINs were provided to Thailand to cover migrants in 26 provinces, with the majority distributed in Tak and Ranong provinces bordering Burma and Chanthaburi and Sa Kaeo provinces bordering Cambodia. PMI also supported delivery costs of LLINs through mass distribution to reach households, information, education, communication (IEC)/BCC to promote use of LLINs and treated material/hammock nets in the focus areas.

Support for Lao PDR has been in response to the outbreaks in the five southern provinces. With FY 2012 funds 30,000 LLINs and an additional 7,000 LLINs have been delivered and distributed.

Progress during the last 12-18 months

In Thailand 60,000 LLINs have been procured with FY 2013 funds for distribution among migrant workers mostly in farms and plantations in border provinces both through PMI-supported malaria control projects and through local malaria clinics.

As southern provinces of Lao PDR continued to report high number of malaria cases, PMI procured 156,100 LLINs with FY 2013 funds for distribution by district and local health centers in the five southern affected provinces which are Saravane, Savannakhet, Champasack, Sekong, and Attapeu where malaria incidence remains relatively high. Supervisors for net distribution reported that polyester LLINs made with softer materials provided by PMI were appropriate for local preference and were well-received by the villagers. CMPE has further requested additional

140,000 LLINs to cover distribution gaps in these provinces. These LLINs will be procured with FY 2014 funds.

Plans and justification

Further efforts are needed to increase access to LLINs/LLIHNs for hard-to-reach populations, especially mobile and migrant populations, forest goers, and pregnant women. In Thailand, despite the challenges inherent with obtaining accurate population estimates of mobile workers and migrants at risk for malaria, the NMCP is giving priority to mobile and migrant populations via distribution of LLIHNs. PMI's procurement of such nets for Thailand is limited and complements nets procured with other sources. In the past, Thailand distributed approximately 100,000 LLINs per year to migrants who presented at health facilities with fever. With Global Fund support ending in 2016, LLINs and LLIHNs will be procured for Thailand if urgent gaps are identified and upon government request, as has been the case in previous years.

PMI will work closely with the CMPE of Lao PDR to ensure sufficient LLINs are available for those most at risk (including pregnant women) and can adjust quantities between countries in the region in 2016 to fill any gaps.

Proposed activities with FY 2016 funding: ($790,000)

- **Procurement and distribution of LLINs and LLIHNs:** Although the GMS countries have funding from the Global Fund to cover most LLIN needs; support post-2016 in Thailand and Laos is uncertain. Therefore, PMI will procure approximately 175,000 LLINs and hammock nets for Thailand and other countries in the region to fill ITN gaps, particularly for migrant, mobile workers and pregnant women, in high endemic areas. ($615,000, Regional)

- **Community-level support for distribution of LLINs:** PMI will support transport and distribution of LLINs for targeted mobile and migrant population in cross-border regions for vulnerable groups. ($175,000, Regional)

2. **Malaria in pregnancy**

NMCP/PMI objectives

The 2012 Thailand Malaria Survey reported an overall PCR malaria prevalence of 0.1% and none of the positives were pregnant women. Given the very low prevalence of malaria, intermittent preventive treatment for pregnant women (IPTp) is not recommended and has not been implemented. PMI, therefore, supports a two-pronged approach to reduce the burden of malaria infection among pregnant women including provision of LLINs and effective case management of malaria and anemia. The NMCP strategy supports distribution of LLINs to households in malaria risk areas. According to the Thailand Malaria Survey, 89% of pregnant women slept under a net, but only 36% used an ITN. PMI has supported BCC activities to encourage people at risk to use LLINs rather than conventional bed nets. These BCC activities are conducted jointly with distribution campaigns in the border focus areas.

Pregnant women with suspected malaria are referred to a hospital for malaria diagnosis and treatment. First-line treatment for *P. falciparum* is quinine in the first trimester and artesunate-mefloquine in the second and third trimesters. *P. vivax* is treated with chloroquine in all trimesters. There is no policy to prevent vivax relapses during pregnancy. ANC attendance is very high in Thailand (99%) and most pregnant women complete the recommended four visits (80%).

Progress since PMI was launched

Following an MIP assessment in 2011, PMI provided support to Ministries of Health to revise policies especially for areas of confirmed artemisinin resistance, ensuring integration of malaria in pregnancy across relevant national programs and improving data on pregnant malaria patients at all health system levels. The assessment found that malaria programs focused on elimination and containment of artemisinin resistance have ignored the role of pregnant women (with no policy of how to manage MIP in the Tier I areas) and that data on the true burden of the disease are not often available (especially from areas where malaria transmission is highest and pregnant women are most at risk). With FY 2013 funding, PMI is supporting an assessment of MIP policies, guidelines, and practices in Laos in both high and low malaria transmission settings. This assessment will complement the 2011 MIP assessment conducted for Burma, Cambodia, and Thailand. The final report with findings and recommendations is expected to be available in late 2015 for the Lao NMCP and stakeholders in-country. In order to further strengthen MIP policies and practices, a regional dissemination workshop focused on the recommendations from all four country MIP assessments is planned with FY 2014 funding for late 2015 in Rangoon, Burma and will bring together both the NMCP and maternal child health focal points.

Progress during the last 12-18 months

In FY 2014, PMI procured 60,000 LLINs which filled gaps in Thailand and provided technical assistance for BCC activities, which included support for translating BCC materials into the appropriate languages of the targeted populations. PMI also supported technical assistance for integrating malaria case management services, including for pregnant women, into routine health services in Thailand.

Proposed activities with FY 2016 funding: ($0)

The Global Fund and Thai MOPH provide the needed support for LLIN distribution and for strengthening case management services. PMI's support for MIP in Thailand and the regional program will focus primarily on support to fill gaps in needed commodities, including LLINs, ACTs, and RDTs. (see ITN and Case Management sections)

3. Case management

Diagnosis and treatment

<u>*NMCP/PMI objectives*</u>

Confirmatory testing, with microscopy or RDTs, is required in all GMS countries before treatment is prescribed. Microscopy is available at most health facilities, while multi-species RDTs are used at the community level. Under the coordination of the WHO Western Pacific Regional Office (WPRO) and with support from PMI, malaria microscopy capacity is strengthened by maintaining a cadre of trainers/supervisors in all GMS countries. Continued attention is needed to ensure that quality microscopy skills are maintained even as malaria incidence wanes.

Thailand's network of malaria clinics and malaria posts using RDTs continues to be the bulwark of service delivery in malaria-endemic areas. Malaria clinics are staffed with well-trained microscopists while malaria posts (Thailand's equivalent of the village malaria worker (VMW) system in place throughout the rest of the GMS) utilize RDTs for diagnosis. Active case detection using microscopy and/or RDTs is carried out in high-risk villages and towns and in the artemisinin resistance containment zones. BVBD, in collaboration with Provincial Health Offices, also is targeting hard-to-reach populations in high-risk border areas through the development of special service facilities where RDTs are available. Some NGOs provide primary health care services, including malaria case management to the 140,000 refugees along the Thai-Burma border.

In Thailand, loose artesunate is combined with mefloquine along with single-dose primaquine (without G6PD screening) as first-line treatment for uncomplicated *P. falciparum*. Chloroquine and primaquine (0.25mg/kg for 14 days) is the first-line treatment for *P. vivax*. Injectable artesunate is available for treatment of severe malaria and generally administered in hospital settings. In light of data from western Thailand showing reduced efficacy of artesunate-mefloquine and more recent results on the efficacy of DHA-Pip, Thailand's National Drug Policy Committee is in the process of registering DHA-Pip and will look to make this treatment alternative available in selected border provinces with waning artesunate + mefloquine efficacy.

In Lao PDR, artemether-lumefantrine is the first-line treatment for *P. falciparum* and *P. vivax* malaria and remains highly efficacious despite the recent finding of K13 artemisinin-resistant genotypes and persistent Day 3 positives in the south.

<u>*Progress since PMI was launched*</u>

A regional slide bank has been maintained with the support of PMI to support regional malaria microscopy training. In Thailand, with FY 2013 funds, 37 health workers at Malaria Posts and Border Malaria Posts, and 87 health workers were trained in malaria diagnosis in Tak and Ranong. A total of 3,371 suspected malaria cases received a diagnostic test in Tak and another 2,651 in Ranong. Of those tested, 352 and 96, respectively, were diagnosed with malaria and treated.

Since 2012, Lao PDR has also seen a large malaria outbreak with more than 95% of reported malaria cases focused in five southern provinces. In response, PMI supported the CMPE by facilitating an emergency distribution of ACTs and RDTs to the southern provinces where malaria incidence remained high after an outbreak that peaked in 2012.

Progress during the last 12-18 months

With PMI support, BVBD conducted an assessment of microscopy quality in malaria clinics in Ranong, Tak, Trat, and Chanthaburi provinces, evaluating parameters of maintenance of laboratory equipment, use of standard protocols, adequacy of laboratory supplies and human resources. The outputs from the assessment resulted in the selection of five malaria clinics to participate in a pilot internal quality control program to enhance microscopy quality. Through close coordination with the Global Fund PR, PMI has transitioned its support of case management activities at Malaria Posts to the Global Fund as of 2014.

With PMI support, six rounds of regional certification trainings for malaria microscopy were carried out in 2014, which reassessed the capacity of national -level trainers in the GMS countries. In June 2014, PMI supported External Competency Assessments for malaria microscopy in Thailand and Lao PDR. Efforts are ongoing to provide support to Thailand for establishment of national slide banks.

PMI's support for therapeutic efficacy studies in the region are described below in the "Surveillance: Drug resistance and therapeutic efficacy studies" section. Briefly, DHA-Pip efficacy testing for *P. falciparum* at two sites in Yunnan Province and four sites in Vietnam in 2014 showed 100% adequate clinical and parasitological response (ACPR). Thailand is currently testing the efficacy of artesunate+mefloquine in three sites and DHA-Pip in one site in Kanchanaburi. Lao PDR is testing artemether-lumefantrine in three sites with preliminary results from Sekong showing high Day 3 positives. Thailand is also conducting chloroquine efficacy testing against *P. vivax* in three sites.

Plans and justification

In Thailand and Lao PDR, the majority of the case management commodities are procured through their respective country Global Fund grants. Thus, PMI's commodity strategy will focus on procuring a limited quantity of RDTs and ACTs to fill unanticipated regional gaps and to respond to malaria outbreaks. PMI will continue to support refresher training of existing laboratory staff and health workers in the performance and use of malaria microscopy and RDTs – integrating malaria case management into routine services where feasible, and strengthening quality assurance systems. In addition, PMI will continue its support for the regional accreditation training and for maintaining the regional slide bank, to ensure that each country has highly skilled trainers/supervisors to oversee diagnostic quality assurance. In accordance with WHO recommendations, standardized and validated slide banks are required for training as well as for accrediting senior microscopists.

Proposed activities with FY 2016 funding: ($176,000)

- **Procure RDTs and microscopy supplies.** PMI will continue to fill gaps in country requirements by procuring multi-species RDTs and reagents and supplies for microscopy, particularly for migrant and mobile populations in PMI focus areas. This will include up to 67,500 RDTs as need arises. ($50,000, Regional)

- **Training and accreditation for microscopy:** PMI will continue support for the training and accreditation of supervisors of malaria microscopy throughout the GMS, maintenance of regional and national slide banks, and maintenance of microscopes. ($90,000, Regional)

- **Procurement of antimalarials.** PMI will procure approximately 23,000 ACTs to reach migrants and to fill regional gaps and outbreaks. ($36,000, Regional)

Pharmaceutical management

NMCP/PMI objectives

Effective malaria case management requires that efficacious, high-quality antimalarials are available and used by both providers and patients according to national guidelines. The availability and use of quality antimalarial medicines, diagnostics, and preventive commodities is a top priority for PMI.

In order to achieve the goal of early diagnosis and treatment of malaria cases in Thailand, the NMCP manages the delivery of commodities to facilities, particularly to the public sector malaria clinics and posts. With Global Fund support, BVBD, PHOs, and District Health Offices (DHOs) have been strengthened to ensure that commodities are well-monitored and distributed to provinces and districts. When there are problems with stock availability, antimalarial drugs are exchanged between facilities and districts. Though the principle of "first expired first out" is being applied, nearly expired drugs and nearly expired RDTs have been found at malaria posts in border areas. The Thai Malaria Program Review in 2012 found that logistics and pharmaceutical management systems in the border provinces, particularly reaching migrant and mobile populations, need improvement. The review also recommended consideration of a stockpile for medicines and diagnostics for potential epidemics. To ensure that the management of malaria drugs and RDTs are kept updated, BVBD began including stock balances into the national malaria reporting system, Biomedical and Public Health Informatics.

In Lao PDR, health infrastructure and supply chain systems are relatively weak. Generally, the Procurement Unit of the Global Fund Principal Recipient procures most of the malaria commodities, according to a forecast provided by the Center for Malariology, Parasitology, and Entomology (CMPE). The pharmaceuticals are stored with the Medical Products Supply Center (MPSC) within the Ministry of Health. Once these are delivered to a warehouse in the capital, the medications and other supplies are then distributed to the provinces per the program's recommendations. The provinces subsequently supply the districts that supply the health centers that then ultimately provide commodities to the village health workers.

Although the Global Fund provided support to renovate part of the MPSC building, significant quantities of expired commodities that needed disposal have been observed at the MPSC and there seemed to be lack of clear guidance about how to manage expired commodities. MPSC has been working with CHAI to pilot and scale up mSupply in the central warehouse and selected regional warehouses.

Progress since PMI was launched

PMI is providing support to strengthen pharmaceutical management and supply chain systems in the region through the procurement of supplies and strengthening the in-country systems that manage them. Activities are organized around improving system performance and visibility to ensure that malaria products are available when and where they are needed, strengthening in-country supply systems and enhancing the capacity for effective management of malaria commodity supply chain. PMI has supported strengthening national counterparts' abilities to provide supply chain forecasting and monitoring data and has also supported the placing of a regional logistics advisor based in Phnom Penh, Cambodia to provide technical assistance toward the compiling, analyzing, and dissemination of supply chain information. The PMI-supported assessment conducted in March 2014 in Thailand revealed that although there are some challenges in the pharmaceutical management and supply system, overall capacity and performance is strong. In contrast, an assessment carried out by PMI in 2013 in Lao PDR found that stockouts of RDTs and ACTs were common due to difficulty in transport and communication systems from lower level to provincial and national level. The challenges and limitations included delays in reporting, completeness, and collection of data.

PMI has been monitoring regional malaria commodity pipelines so potential bottlenecks in procurement and distribution of malaria commodities (including Global Fund-financed commodities) can be quickly addressed and availability of key commodities ensured. A preliminary assessment of quantification processes in some GMS countries has contributed to a better understanding of the NMCP's capabilities to monitoring commodities, resources, and gaps. The regionally-based technical advisor is providing information on malaria commodity pipelines for the region, analyzing potential gaps and weaknesses, as well as supporting various supply chain management activities on behalf of partners.

Progress during the last 12-18 months

Responding to the increase of malaria cases in southern provinces of Lao PDR, PMI provided technical assistance to assess the status of malaria drugs and RDTs at district and health center levels in the endemic provinces. Subsequently, PMI provided support for a consultant to work closely with CMPE staff and develop a Logistic Malaria Information System (LMIS) to strengthen reporting of malaria commodities stock from district to national levels. With FY 2015 funds, PMI provided technical assistance support to improve data use for forecasting of commodities and to identify and address bottlenecks in data and logistics management at the provincial and district. In addition, as a short-term measure, PMI arranged "last mile delivery support" to CMPE during 2014 to transport ACTs and RDTs procured by PMI to district hospitals and health centers in five highly affected provinces in the south of the country.

In 2015, PMI also coordinated the hiring of a malaria supply chain advisor to support CMPE with funding from the US 5% Initiative to build capacity in the area of procurement and supply chain management of malaria commodities, and to improve the ability of CMPE to integrate into the overall national procurement and supply chain management processes. The recently hired advisor will focus on national and provincial level coordination with other stakeholders, including the Global Fund and CHAI and ensure that the LMIS tools are harmonized with the national information systems.

Plans and justification

PMI will continue to support strengthening pharmaceutical management and supply chain systems in the region through the procurement of supplies and strengthening the in-country systems that manage them with a focus on Lao PDR. PMI will continue to coordinate closely with the MOH, other donors and partners (e.g. the Global Fund and CHAI) to improve the supply chain management systems at all levels focusing on quality issues, stockouts, expiries and their destruction, product optimization, storage, and support/development of future procurement and supply chain management plans.

In FY 2016, there are no plans for PMI funding to provide dedicated technical assistance for pharmaceutical management in Thailand. PMI will continue to work regionally to improve coordination and strengthen capacity for forecasting, quantification, management, and distribution, and be ready to respond to outbreaks or commodity gaps as required. In Lao PDR, PMI will continue to coordinate the supply chain technical assistance funded by the US 5% Initiative, depending on the availability of future funds.

Proposed activities with FY 2016 funding: ($0)

There are no proposed pharmaceutical management activities in FY 2016.

Drug quality

NMCP/PMI objectives

The use of poor quality medicines may lead to treatment failures, increased morbidity and mortality, and the development of drug resistance. The availability of high-quality antimalarials and removal of substandard drugs are essential to mitigating drug resistance in the region. All governments of the region have banned the import of oral artemisinin monotherapy and are taking additional measures to be able to detect and remove poor quality drugs both in the private as well as the public sector.

PMI has provided leadership in the GMS to improve the quality of antimalarial drugs. Through the support of the USG and other donors, the countries in the GMS have developed extensive networks of sentinel sites using portable drug quality testing kits (Minilabs®). PMI has also supported building capacity and strengthening the national drug quality laboratories in the region with a focus on achieving ISO-17025 laboratory accreditation. In addition, PMI has worked with national food and drug administrations, medicine regulatory agencies, and other authorities to develop appropriate enforcement approaches to regulate the drug industry. The countries also benefit from training obtained through the Asian Network of Excellence in Quality Assurance of Medicines, a network of university pharmaceutical programs providing technical assistance within the region to develop national capacities for quality assurance/quality control (QA/QC), good manufacturing practices, and bioavailability testing.

Progress since PMI was launched

PMI has provided tremendous support towards establishing a drug quality network in the GMS, periodically collecting field specimens for monitoring of drug quality and working with national and international authorities, and providing data to national and international authorities to take enforcement actions. Enforcement actions against violators have included suspension and revocation of operation licenses, closures of medicine outlets, fines, arrests of perpetrators, delisting of products from approved registration and banning of imports, product recalls, and confiscation and disposal of non-conforming products. PMI has supported site visits to Burma, Cambodia, Lao PDR, Thailand, and Viet Nam to provide needed reagents, reference standards, standard national formularies, and other essential supplies. PMI has also supported the provision of technical guidance to these countries as appropriate and follow up of any actions taken (e.g., in Lao PDR, issuing regulatory notices, and fining and educating violators).

PMI has also strengthened medicine quality assurance systems through in-country capacity building. PMI continues to support provision of technical assistance to the National Health Products Quality Control Center's (NHQC) laboratories through advanced analytical trainings, provision of equipment and supplies, and ongoing good laboratory practices assistance to attain accreditation by the International Organization for Standardization (ISO). For example, it has provided technical assistance to continue to strengthen the capacity of the Lao Food and Drug Quality Control Laboratory Center toward ISO 17025 accreditation, as well as to strengthen Chulalongkorn University in Thailand's Pharmaceutical Technology Service Center toward WHO Prequalification. With PMI support, the Viet Nam National Institute of Drug Quality Control and Thailand Bureau of Drug and Narcotics laboratories have achieved WHO prequalification status.

Progress during the last 12-18 months

PMI has continued to support a drug quality network in the GMS with periodic collection of drugs for monitoring of drug quality. Although three sentinel sites in Lao PDR and four sites in Thailand are supported by PMI currently, there are many challenges to conducting post-market surveillance including difficulties with sampling, lengthy confirmatory testing, and limited enforcement capacity.

Over the last two years, PMI has established two regional mechanisms to promote information-sharing among GMS countries. The Build Regional Expertise in Medicines Regulation and Enforcement (BREMERE) mechanism was designed to increase regional cooperation and access to a pool of experts in medicines regulation to address the medicines quality issues and problems in the region. Through this mechanism, country medicine regulatory agencies and other law enforcement agencies have access to a regional platform through which they can share information for effective enforcement in a timely manner. BREMERE expands access beyond national and regional levels by working in partnership with WHO (Southeast Asia Regional Office and WPRO), INTERPOL, ASEAN, and national authorities. The second mechanism is the Asia Pacific Network of Official Medicines Control Laboratories, which assists with QA/QC laboratories in the region to support regulatory authorities in controlling the quality of antimalarial medications available on the market. This network parallels other successful Official Medicines Control Laboratories networks worldwide.

PMI recently supported a regional drug quality assessment, conducted in March 2014, to take a closer look at what has been achieved in the last decade and where donors should focus in years to come, including but not limited to PMI support. The assessment has highlighted what PMI has already known regarding access to good quality medicines in private sector outlets. Based on the findings and recommendations of the assessment report, PMI will continue to support strengthening of drug monitoring surveillance in select countries and national capacity building throughout the region.

Plans and justification

Due to challenges with post-market surveillance and recent data that the availability of poor quality drugs has decreased in recent years, PMI will focus its support to working with the national pharmaceutical reference laboratories to strengthen their capacity to conduct the necessary laboratory analyses for national drug quality monitoring. This support will focus on only Thailand as Lao PDR has already obtained ISO certification.

Proposed activities with FY 2016 funding: ($50,000)

- **Drug quality assurance:** PMI will strengthen capacity of national quality control laboratories by supporting technical assistance to the national pharmaceutical reference laboratory in Thailand in order to obtain ISO 17025 certification by 2017. ($50,000, Thailand)

4. **Health system strengthening and capacity building**

NMCP/PMI objectives

PMI supports a broad array of health system strengthening activities which cut across intervention areas, such as training of health workers, supply chain management and health information systems strengthening, drug quality monitoring, and NCMP capacity building. Particularly as the malaria burden continues to decline towards malaria elimination, healthcare capacities for malaria in GMS countries face many challenges including the shortage of skilled health workers and technical staff, high turnover, and lack of motivation among trained staff in remote and inaccessible areas. Decentralization of the health care system and integration of malaria control into general health services place an additional management burden on the provincial and district levels.

Progress since PMI was launched

PMI has provided long-standing support to strengthen regional technical capacity through ACTMalaria. ACTMalaria is an inter-country training and communication network which includes NMCPs of Bangladesh, Cambodia, China, Republic of Indonesia, Lao PDR, Malaysia, Burma, Philippines, Thailand, Timor-Leste, and Viet Nam. ACTMalaria has been a primary mechanism for building technical and management capacity and facilitating information exchange among its member countries. Through PMI's support of this regional training and capacity building network, national programs have successfully leveraged domestic and/or Global Fund resources to support participation in these training opportunities. ACTMalaria is also a key partner in capacity building within the Asian Pacific Malaria Elimination Network which is supported by DFAT. While continuing their work with established courses (e.g. the Management of Malaria Field Operations (MMFO), Quality Assurance for Diagnostics, and Integrated Vector Management), ACTMalaria explores opportunities to develop new curricula as identified by the executive board of the eleven member NMCPs. It should be noted that Integrated Vector Management (IVM) training is organized by the Ministry of Health, Malaysia; however, ACTMalaria, through support from PMI, provides technical assistance and supports some participants to attend this regional training which focuses on methods and approaches for integrating vector control and vector management.

Progress during the last 12-18 months

In 2014, PMI supported regional training courses to build the capacity of NMCPs in malaria management and field operations, M&E, diagnostics and case management and integrated vector management. Technical assistance has been provided for updating and refining curricula which include Integrated Vector Management, Vector Control for Elimination, Malaria Elimination and Surveillance, and MMFO training courses. To assess the impact of these trainings for the participants in their respective roles and responsibilities after the training, an external evaluation (Level 3: on-the-job application or transfer of learning) was commissioned in September 2012. The main findings from this evaluation were that, despite some attrition, those participants who have remained with the malaria programs have seen improvements in their skills and capacity to manage malaria programs as well as greater self-confidence, improved communication especially in English, and other interpersonal skills.

Plans and justification

Strengthening national program capacity is a critical component of the PMI strategy. PMI will continue to support national and regional capacity-building and training efforts on program management, quality assurance/quality control for diagnostics, M&E, and surveillance. Support for improving data quality and use of strategic information in Lao PDR will be provided. PMI-supported trainings are performance-based, tailored to the needs of the participants, and led by NMCPs.

Proposed activities with FY 2016 funding: ($320,000)

- **Strengthen NMCP capacity**: PMI will support coordination and facilitation of regional training courses, including MMFO for program managers. ($200,000, Regional)

- **Support for strategic information**: PMI will support strengthening the CMPE's capacity for data management and use, surveillance, and using epidemiological data to inform forecasting and procurement through provision of a local advisor in Lao PDR. ($120,000, Regional)

Table 6: Health Systems Strengthening Activities

HSS Building Block	Technical Area	Description of Activity
Health Services	Case Management	Improve QA systems to monitor the quality of laboratory diagnostic service; training and supervision for health staff and village malaria workers to provide malaria services
Health Workforce	Health Systems Strengthening	Build, through training and technical assistance, host country managerial and leadership capacity for effective malaria control through courses such as MMFO
Health Information	Monitoring and Evaluation	Strengthen disease surveillance systems to improve decision-making, planning, forecasting, and program management; provide support and technical assistance to improve M&E capacity at national and subnational levels
Essential Medical Products, Vaccines, and Technologies	Case Management	Support technical assistance for improved forecasting, procurement, quality control, storage and distribution of malaria commodities, such as ITNs, ACTs, and RDTs in Lao PDR

5. Behavior change communication

NMCP/PMI objectives

Thailand attracts migrant workers from neighboring countries, particularly from Burma and Cambodia. Approximately half of the malaria cases in Thailand are among migrant workers recorded as those who have resided in Thailand for longer than 6 months (M1) or less (M2). Access to prevention and treatment services has been improved through LLIN distribution and community-based services provided by malaria posts along border areas. The majority of these workers are laborers in farms, fruit orchards, and plantations. Their employers are important gate keepers for their access and movement.

Both the Global Fund Round 10/SSF and the Global Fund RAI grants (2014-2016) aim to provide comprehensive BCC, community mobilization, and access to health services for both Thai people and migrants residing in malaria transmission zones in 44 provinces in Thailand that border with neighboring countries. The BVBD developed a framework for BCC for the Thai population that encourages acceptance of IRS, prompt treatment-seeking behaviors, drug adherence, use of LLINs, and use of LLIHNs when staying outdoors. The BCC component targeting displaced Burmese along the Thai-Burmese border and other migrant populations in Thailand along border provinces is implemented by NGOs.

Progress since PMI was launched

PMI has supported the BVBD to increase the availability of multilingual BCC materials appropriate for transnational migrants from other GMS countries to increase health- seeking behaviors and treatment compliance. In Thailand, PMI has taken advantage of regionalist cross-border presence by bringing personnel and BCC staff from Burma and Cambodia to assist in training of migrant malaria volunteers in border provinces.

Progress during the last 12-18 months

With FY 2013 and FY 2014 funding for Thailand, PMI-supported project staff and volunteers conducted outreach and assisted Thai malaria workers during case investigations. Support was also provided for training of health staff and facilitators for bilingual case management. The mid-term evaluation of the regional PMI-supported, CAP-Malaria project in 2014 found that bilingual signs at visited border crossings were clear and helped migrants locate nearby services.

The BCC materials have been developed and, moving forward, BVBD will take over activities to maintain and update them. PMI will continue working with WHO and relevant NMCPs in harmonizing and coordinating BCC messages across the region for migrant workers.

Additionally, with FY 2013 funding, PMI and WHO jointly conducted a regional BCC assessment focusing on border areas of Burma, Thailand, Cambodia, and Lao PDR. The assessment reviewed availability of BCC materials, existing BCC activities, and access to LLINs and malaria treatment among migrant and mobile populations. Preliminary results of this assessment found that migrant population are diverse in regards to their malaria knowledge and perceptions. In some rural areas, misconceptions about the causes of malaria (such as the belief that malaria is caused by drinking unclean water or eating certain fruits) still persist. The majority of those interviewed mentioned that interpersonal communication and health education sessions remain the most preferred, trusted, and effective communication channels. Therefore, BCC interventions and channels for communication should be tailored. Once the report is finalized, PMI will collaborate with partners to review and address findings and recommendations through wide dissemination.

Plans and justification

With support for BCC already being provided by the Global Fund and the Thai MOPH, no specific funding is allocated for BCC. However, to the extent possible, PMI will continue to provide technical support and facilitate communication strategies and use of appropriate BCC approaches among migrant and at-risk populations.

Proposed activities with FY 2016 funding: ($0)

PMI supports integration of BCC activities in the delivery of malaria services (e.g., distribution of LLINs and case management), and these are covered under the respective intervention areas.

6. Monitoring and evaluation

NMCP/PMI objectives

All countries in the GMS currently have either national or sub-national malaria elimination goals as part of their national malaria strategy. Thailand's 2011-2016 National Strategic Plan for Malaria Control and Elimination sets as their target malaria elimination in 95% of the country by the year 2020. Lao PDR's National Strategy for Malaria Control and Pre-Elimination has set the goal of reducing incidence and deaths and eliminating malaria in 6 provinces in the north by 2020. Viet Nam's National Strategic Plan aims to reduce morbidity and mortality and achieve malaria elimination in 40 out of 63 provinces by 2020.

A timely and responsive surveillance system is critical for NMCPs to move from the control to the elimination phase, and to be able to detect, investigate, and respond to every malaria case. Malaria surveillance has been integrated into the Health Management Information Systems (HMIS) in all six GMS countries. However, the HMIS and its capacity in the GMS vary widely from paper to web-based surveillance and from passive case detection (of cases that may or may not be parasitologically confirmed) to active case detection in some places (e.g. China and Thailand). Most HMIS in the region aggregate malaria data and do not capture adequate information for malaria elimination, and will likely require complementary case-based malaria information or reporting systems.

The inclusion of malaria data from the private sector is a critical element for malaria elimination, particularly in a region where a significant proportion of individuals seek services from these largely unregulated outlets and clinics. This is the case in most GMS countries with the exception of Thailand where antimalarial drugs are not allowed to be sold in pharmacies or private clinics. More effort will be needed to work with the private sector to consolidate data as part of one national surveillance system. The long-term goal is to have a single surveillance system that incorporates both data from public and private sectors.

Limitations of current surveillance systems in the GMS include delays and incompleteness of reports and the collection of data only from the public sector. Most programs struggle to collect timely data from peripheral settings, such as from community-level volunteers, the private sector, the military, and migrants. Routine surveillance challenges in the region include a lack of adequate feedback and supervision, poor information technology infrastructures limiting timely reporting of data, and weak capacity for data management and analysis, especially at the periphery. Often the data are not disaggregated by factors that are epidemiologically relevant (e.g. age, gender, pregnancy status, ethnicity, migrant status, or occupation). These weaknesses were highlighted in the delay of identifying malaria outbreaks in the southern provinces of Lao PDR reporting caseloads four to eight times the previous year's levels, and appearing to have spread to neighboring Thailand and Cambodia. Weak reporting systems preventing timely detection of the increases in malaria cases, increased mobilization of migrant workers to the area, a lapse in LLIN distributions in 2010 due to procurement delays by the Global Fund, and a prolonged rainy season in 2011 may have been contributing factors in the spike in cases in southern Laos.

Progress since PMI was launched

Capacity for M&E in the GMS has generally improved, but has largely been driven by reporting requirements to donors such as the Global Fund. However, there have been various attempts to harmonize and streamline M&E efforts within country programs, as well as for the GMS. The GMS has experienced various iterations of regional monitoring and evaluation frameworks for malaria beginning with the Kunming Indicators in 1999 and more recently the Bi-Regional Malaria Indicator Framework in 2011. The Bi-Regional Malaria Indicator Framework aimed to develop a comprehensive set of indicators for malaria control and elimination in the GMS countries. It also provided guidance on the M&E of programmatic responses to these challenges by outlining a conceptual framework, and identifying relevant indicators useful for improving program management.

Recognizing the importance of M&E and surveillance, PMI has provided technical assistance to the development of National M&E Plans for Thailand, Lao PDR, and Viet Nam. Furthermore, to assist NMCPs to adopt the regional M&E indicators and to build M&E capacity, PMI supported a regional M&E course which was conducted in September 2012. This two-week training course aimed to train a cadre of M&E experts and trainers within each country who would be able to adapt the curriculum to their country context and conduct national and sub-national trainings. Following the training, Lao PDR was the first country to adapt the curriculum to their national context and conducted provincial-level trainings with funding from other sources.

There have been some population-based surveys conducted in the GMS to monitor progress on malaria interventions. Thailand completed its first national malaria survey in 2013, which showed very low parasitemia and gaps in knowledge and LLIN use. Other surveys in the region included Lao PDR's Social Indicator Survey (2011-2012) with a malaria module and Viet Nam's Multiple Indicator Cluster Survey in 2011 which collected some data on mosquito net use.

Table 7: Monitoring and Evaluation table (Surveys conducted in Thailand, Lao PDR, and Viet Nam)

Data Source	Year							
	2010	2011	2012	2013	2014	2015	2016	2017
House-hold Surveys		Lao PDR LSIS* (2011-12) Viet Nam MICS* (2011)	Thai CAP-Malaria baseline	Thai National Malaria Survey* (2012-2013)	Viet Nam MICS* (2013-2014)	Thai KAP Survey*	Lao PDR LSIS Survey*	
Other Surveys	Migrant RDS survey at Thai-Cambodia border*		Migrant RDS survey at Thai-Burma border		Lao-Cambodia-Viet Nam border screening survey*			
Other Data Sources		Ento monitoring	Ento monitoring	Ento monitoring	Ento monitoring	Ento monitoring	Ento monitoring	Ento monitoring
	TES (USAID)	TES (PMI)	TES (PMI)	TES (PMI)	TES (PMI)	TES (PMI)	TES (PMI)	TES (PMI)
		Drug Quality Monitoring	Drug Quality Monitoring	Drug Quality Monitoring	Drug Quality Monitoring	Drug Quality Monitoring	Drug Quality Monitoring	Drug Quality Monitoring
		TRaC*	TRaC*	TRaC*				

* Not PMI-supported

Furthermore, malaria data from migrants and mobile populations have been difficult to ascertain as traditional survey methods often miss this population and the quality of routine surveillance data is variable. PMI-supported respondent-driven sampling (RDS) surveys, a methodology used often with hidden populations, were conducted amongst Burmese and Cambodian migrants along the Thai borders to ascertain malaria prevention and treatment coverage; these noted very low malaria prevalence and lower ITN utilization among migrants compared to Thai residents.

PMI supported the Mekong Malaria III Monograph which reviewed both epidemiological and entomological data from 2000 to 2010 serving as a benchmark to measure past and future successes. The review also included analyses on relationships with health systems, program costs and financing, community involvement, private sector engagement, and cross-border collaboration for all the countries in the GMS. This analytical review also projected regional trends in socio-economic development, migration, and other factors likely to affect malaria transmission and ultimately malaria elimination.

Progress during the last 12-18 months

PMI continues to be engaged in discussions at country, regional, and global levels on malaria elimination. For example, PMI is a collaborating partner in the Surveillance, Monitoring & Evaluation Technical Expert Group (SME TEG), which is a working group designated as a technical advisory body to harmonize and standardize M&E tools for WHO ERAR monitoring and evaluation, and to facilitate data-sharing among countries, partners, and stakeholders through the development of a regional database. More recently, PMI participated in a Surveillance and Response Working Group of the Asian Pacific Malaria Elimination Network to harmonize indicators and activities for malaria elimination and post-elimination. Attendees included country partners, partner institutions, WHO, and members of the SME TEG.

In Lao PDR, PMI has provided technical support for the development of the National Strategic Plan (2015-2020). PMI has also supported a strategic information advisor in Lao PDR, which has improved the data management and M&E capacity of the national program.

Plans and justification

PMI will focus on the following areas for monitoring, evaluation, and surveillance: 1) ensuring the collection of quality, standardized routine data and survey data that feeds into national surveillance systems, particularly those from rural communities and private sectors; 2) technical assistance for the development and operationalization of national M&E plans; 3) technical support for national/ sub-national surveys; and 4) building national M&E capacity. With the relatively low malaria prevalence and goals of malaria elimination in the region, PMI will emphasize strengthening routine surveillance systems and rely less on large national surveys. Support will be provided to strengthen M&E activities in the PMI focus areas and to strengthen routine data collection at the community level. More specifically, PMI will support technical assistance to improve the NMCP's capacity to analyze and use strategic information, and to evaluate malaria elimination models and activities currently implemented in Thailand. Support for trainings and workshops are also envisioned as part of the technical assistance to build capacity of these important skills amongst NMCP staff.

Proposed activities with FY 2016 funding: ($314,500)

- **Support for M&E activities and surveillance system strengthening**: Technical assistance will be provided to ensure quality routine surveillance particularly in Lao PDR and Thailand; technical assistance to improve M&E, data quality, and use of strategic information and evaluation of malaria elimination models and interventions in Thailand; support will be provided in revising national strategic plans as well as updating national M&E plans. ($200,000, Thailand; $104,500, Regional)

- **Technical assistance on M&E:** A CDC epidemiologist will provide technical assistance with on-going M&E activities and support NMCP's with their M&E plans. ($10,000, Regional)

7. **Surveillance: Drug resistance and therapeutic efficacy studies**

NMCP/PMI objectives

Therapeutic efficacy studies and other drug resistance monitoring methods have played a critical role in the detection of resistance to several classes of malaria drugs. Since 2011, the PMI-supported GMS TES network consists of 46 sentinel sites that are active in the six countries on a rotating basis (Cambodia- 11 sites; China- 3 sites in Yunnan; Lao PDR- 3 sites; Burma- 11 sites; Thailand- 10 sites; Viet Nam- 8 sites). In addition to these TES sites, this network has been expanded and strengthened in the past few years to include chloroquine-resistant *P. vivax* monitoring using funding from other sources such as the Global Fund. Therapeutic efficacy studies have played a crucial role in shaping NMCP treatment policies. In 2008, Thailand's treatment policy shifted from a two-day to a three-day regimen of artesunate-mefloquine in response to suboptimal clinical responses documented in Trat. Recently, BVBD has endorsed shifting to DHA-Pip in response to preliminary data obtained from TES sites along the Thai-Burma border.

In addition to the value of determining clinical outcomes, the TES protocols are also useful for monitoring parasitological markers that may presage inadequate clinical responses. The persistence of parasitemia at the third day after treatment ("Day 3 positives") is being used as a marker of possible foci of artemisinin resistance and could be effectively tracked in settings where prolonged patient follow up may not be feasible. Another benefit of Day 3 positivity as a marker of resistance is that it may be more reflective of inadequate drug responses to the artemisinin component of an ACT regimen. Although there are not yet data to rigorously correlate Day 3 positivity to clinical outcomes, it is generally reassuring that the majority of patients with Day 3 parasitemia will eventually clear parasites.

Progress since PMI was launched

Although 46 sentinel sites throughout the GMS have now been maintained for several years and remain a priority of the NMCPs, the network continues to strive for standardization of methods to ensure that measured efficacy rates can be compared from one location to another. A major goal for the network will be to continue to ensure quality results among all participating sites. Despite the fact that TES present significant logistical and technical challenges and malaria case numbers are declining, PMI will work with the NMCPs to collect quality *in vivo* data.

Figure 10: Map of Day 3 positivity rates in the GMS, 2012 (Source: WHO)

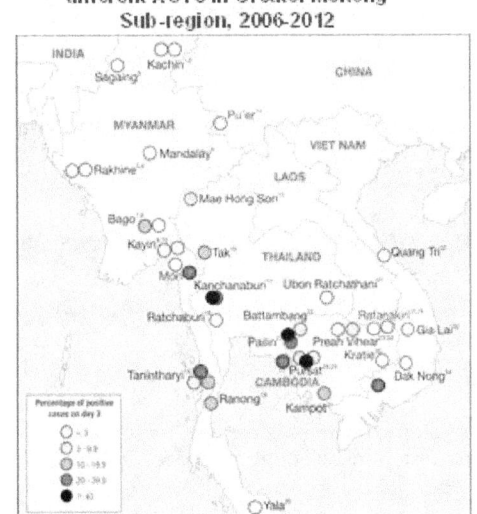

Progress during the last 12-18 months

Analysis of Day 3 positivity data in TES sites was consistent with its role as a harbinger of artemisinin resistance. In Kanchanaburi Province, Thailand, increasing proportions of patients are still positive on Day 3, and in Viet Nam, despite the fact that DHA-Pip efficacy remains high, Day 3 positivity was observed in 15.3% and 11.3% of patients in Binh Phuoc and Gia Lai, respectively.

In February 2014, a new candidate marker for artemisinin resistance was identified[1]. This marker, on the "propeller region" of the K13 *P. falciparum* gene, is associated with both prolonged parasite clearance times and increased IC50s using a specialized *in vitro* drug sensitivity assay specifically developed to detect inhibition of young ring stages of asexual stage parasites. The specific operational role of the K13 mutations in detecting new foci or spreading foci of artemisinin resistance is yet to be determined and more information about other mutations is needed from other sites to validate the epidemiological utility of the marker. Most researchers are not conducting single-nucleotide polymorphism PCRs as there are too many mutations, but are sequencing the domain. Besides K13 mutations, researchers are monitoring other known mutations e.g. PfMDR copy numbers and *cyt b* mutations (markers for mefloquine and atovaquone resistance, respectively), where appropriate, to guide treatment policy.

To report results gathered to date and to plan future TES activities, PMI supported a regional TES meeting in 2014. Key issues identified include a need to strategically prioritize the number and location of future TES surveillance studies, the role of molecular surveillance in the setting of waning malaria burden, differentiating the established role of TES as a rigorous surveillance methodology vs. new initiatives to follow patients up to Day 28 in a broader public health treatment settings, and developing surveillance methods more suited to populations unlikely to be assessed in the context of traditional TES.

Key recommendations from the 2014 TES meeting included:
- Maintain quality TES with current sentinel sites (justification to shift/add sites)
  - Continue TES slide validation by country Level 1 expert
  - Initiate collection of filter paper samples for assays on molecular markers for resistance
- Regularly review TES results for relevance to national drug policy, including data from neighboring or adjacent countries when formulating policy
- Develop correlates of molecular and parasitological markers of resistance with clinical outcomes
- Develop approaches to monitor drug resistance in areas where TES studies are not feasible

---

[1] Ariey, et al. A molecular marker of artemisinin-resistant *Plasmodium falciparum* malaria. Nature 505, 50–55 (2014)

- Continue to build capacity to conduct clinical and laboratory methods to assess drug resistance

Plans and justification

The TES network to monitor antimalarial drug resistance has been instrumental in assisting national programs to update their national treatment policies and guidelines. PMI plans to continue support of therapeutic monitoring in selected sites throughout the region using standardized WHO protocols. PMI will provide enhanced support to molecular detection of K13 mutant genotypes from patients enrolled in TES studies. Other sources of funding for TES sites come from the Global Fund and WHO.

Proposed activities with FY 2016 funding: ($685,000)

- **Regional TES network:** PMI will continue to support the NMCPs to conduct TES at 46 sites across the six countries (sites alternating every two years) including K13 monitoring. Along with testing the current first-line regimens, testing replacement therapies is imperative, especially as countries prepare to update their treatment guidelines. WHO will continue to provide regional coordination and technical assistance to the NMCPs in protocol adaptation, data analysis and dissemination of results (biannual TES meeting), as well as updating national treatment guidelines and implementation support for designated TES sites in Thailand, Lao PDR, China and Viet Nam. ($435,000, Regional; $150,000, Thailand)

- **Technical assistance to conduct TES in Thailand:** PMI will provide technical assistance support to the NMCP to ensure that TES is conducted in compliance with International Conference for Harmonization Good Clinical Practice guidance in Thailand. ($100,000, Thailand)

8. Surveillance: Entomology

NMCP/PMI objectives

As rapid ecologic changes occur with economic development, deforestation, and scale-up of LLINs in the GMS, there are two important priorities: 1) mapping of vectors in areas where epidemiologic data indicate that malaria transmission continues to occur and 2) improved surveillance for insecticide resistance. The forested areas and possibly some plantations in the GMS are home to the region's most efficient malaria vector, *An. dirus*, with second major vectors, *An. minimus* and *An. maculatus*, found in the forest and forest-fringe areas and possibly in the new orchard and rubber plantation ecologies. Beyond these major vectors, there are a plethora of secondary vectors, whose importance in the rapidly changing ecology of the region is still largely unknown. Unlike the TES network, the entomological surveillance undertaken by NMCPs and some foundations, universities and research institutions within each of the GMS countries is often uncoordinated and the results are not widely disseminated. Throughout the region, surveys on vector bionomics and for insecticide resistance need to be better correlated with malaria transmission and epidemiological data.

61

In the cross-border focus areas, where PMI and other donors are supporting efforts to scale up LLINs, NMCPs need to monitor and evaluate a few basic entomological parameters. The proper approach towards entomologic surveillance is immensely complicated by the shifting ecology of forest habitats, the complexity of vector bionomics and behavior and the variable overlying malaria epidemiology as programs shift from control to elimination on a subnational scale.

Progress since PMI was launched

Thailand's workforce of entomologists is a particular strength, with a highly trained technical staff. As with other malaria specific skills, technical expertise will become more challenging as malaria burden wanes and fiscal concerns encourage integration of vertical programs into larger structures. PMI continues to support regional strengthening of entomologic surveillance, insecticide resistance monitoring, and development and evaluation of methods to interrupt outdoor transmission in the region.

Working in collaboration with WHO and RBM, PMI continues assisting with coordination of personnel and resources to strengthen entomologic monitoring in the region. PMI continues to engage with the Japan International Cooperation Agency (JICA), Mahidol University, the Institute of Tropical Medicine Antwerp, and the AFRIMS to strengthen entomologic capacity in the region.

Progress during the last 12-18 months

In 2014, with PMI support, BVBD conducted vector bionomic studies in Kraburi District, Ranong Province, using a combination of indoor human landing captures, animal baits, and CDC light traps. In human landing captures, the major anopheline species was *An. barbirostris* (11% of all species), while animal landing studies detected *An. barbirostris, An. campestris,* and *An. hyrcanus gr.*, comprising 11, 5, and 10% of all species, respectively. The CDC light trap detected only a small fraction of anopheline species.

BVBD also conducted LLIN efficacy tests using the traditional cone bioassay from nets retrieved from the same area on four year old nets. Testing of 24 nets showed that knock down rates at 15 and 60 minutes averaged 46.7% and 85.3%, respectively, while 24-hour mortality averaged 74.3%. However, only 57% of LLINs tested were found effective in killing test strains with a frequency of 80% or greater. PMI will continue to provide technical support to BVBD's LLIN longevity studies to best inform LLIN durability and replacement strategies.

Plans and justification

The considerable variation of anopheline distribution from site to site makes interpretation of the entomological data challenging. Given that there are sites for entomological surveillance which are being conducted by NMCPs with other resources such as funding from the Global Fund, PMI will provide technical assistance for entomological monitoring and surveillance. For insecticide resistance, data from GMS are uncommon compared to the fine-scale data available for drug resistance. Thus, development of better networks for insecticide surveillance is needed. Finally, the ability of programs to conduct entomological surveys to better understand malaria risk in particular ecological zones requires additional support. For the coming year, the CDC Entomology Branch will conduct TDYs to the region to consult with programs and facilitate coordination of support for these activities supported by the Global Fund, JICA, PMI, and the research community. Coordination efforts both across countries and across partners will be emphasized. PMI/Mekong aims to assist with regional coordination of entomological activities through direct engagement of CDC entomology branch staff in discussions with NMCPs to ensure rational implementation of entomological surveys related to transmission, insecticide resistance, and LLIN durability; through regional networks such as Asia Pacific Malaria Elimination Network (APMEN), which coordinates information-sharing and training related to insecticide resistance in the region; and through ACTMalaria, which will assist in organization of regional entomological capacity trainings.

Proposed activities with FY 2016 funding: ($14,500)

- **Technical support for entomology.** One TDY from a CDC entomologist is planned to provide technical assistance to Thailand and will emphasize regional planning and coordination. ($14,500)

9. Operational research

NMCP/PMI objectives

Malaria elimination is now a priority for Thailand's BVBD, and has identified the need to better improve its strategy and interventions to reach its mobile and migrant populations in the context of achieving malaria elimination within its borders. Moreover, BVBD seeks to develop a sustainable and resourced package of interventions to achieve malaria elimination in Thailand.

In Lao PDR, the national malaria strategy has prioritized operational research in case management, particularly with regard to G6PD mapping and screening, as well as the epidemiology of malaria among mobile workers in development projects and forest-goers.

Progress since PMI was launched

To identify the priority OR questions for the GMS, an OR symposium was convened for the sub-region. Prior to the symposium, country level assessments of their current OR activities, priorities, and gaps were identified and synthesized for the regional meeting. This regional symposium facilitated the development of an OR framework for malaria control and elimination in the GMS, by identifying common regional malaria research priorities, facilitating linkages across the region, and promoting greater coordination and sharing of findings. The symposium identified several priority questions for six topic areas (vector control and prevention, case management, *P. vivax* and G6PD, vulnerable populations, M&E and surveillance, and health systems and private sector).

In 2011, USAID supported a Respondent-Driven Sampling study in Ranong, Thailand which looked to better understand migrant mobility, treatment-seeking behaviors, and malaria burden among Burmese migrants living and working in Ranong. The study showed that malaria burden was low among these sedentary immigrant populations, and their risk for transporting malaria from Burma was fairly limited.

Progress during the last 12-18 months

There were no PMI-supported OR activities in Thailand or Lao PDR during the last 12-18 months.

Plans and justification:

There are no operational research activities planned with FY 2016 funding.

10. Staffing and administration

One health professional will serve as a resident advisor to oversee PMI in the Mekong. In addition, one Foreign Service National (FSN) works as part of the PMI team. All PMI staff members are led by the USAID Mission Director or his/her designee in country. The PMI team shares responsibility for development and implementation of PMI strategies and work plans, coordination with national authorities, managing collaborating agencies, and supervising day-to-day activities. Candidates for resident advisor positions (whether initial hires or replacements) will be evaluated and/or interviewed jointly by USAID and CDC, and both agencies will be involved in hiring decisions, with the final decision made by the individual agency.

The PMI professional staff work together to oversee all technical and administrative aspects of PMI, including finalizing details of the project design, implementing malaria prevention and treatment activities, monitoring and evaluation of outcomes and impact, reporting of results, and providing guidance to PMI partners.

The PMI lead in country is the USAID Mission Director. The day-to-day lead for PMI is delegated to the USAID Health Office Director and thus the resident advisor reports to the USAID Health Office Director for day-to-day leadership. The technical expertise housed in Atlanta and Washington guides PMI programmatic efforts.

The PMI resident advisor is based within the USAID health office and is expected to spend approximately half their time sitting with and providing technical assistance to the national malaria control programs and partners.

Locally-hired staff to support PMI activities either in Ministries or in USAID will be approved by the USAID Mission Director. Because of the need to adhere to specific country policies and USAID accounting regulations, any transfer of PMI funds directly to Ministries or host governments will need to be approved by the USAID Mission Director and Controller, in addition to the US Global Malaria Coordinator.

Proposed activities with FY 2016 funding: ($650,000)

- Support for USAID/PMI Resident Advisor and FSN (including 100% FSN and in-country support, administrative costs). ($590,000)

- Travel cost support for regional TDYs from RDMA RAs and FSN. ($60,000)

Table 1: Budget Breakdown by Mechanism

President's Malaria Initiative – *Thailand/Regional*

Planned Malaria Obligations for FY 2016

Mechanism	Geographic Area	Activity	Budget ($)	%
TBD- Supply Chain Contract	Regional	Procurement of LLINs/LLIHNs, RDTs, ACTs to fill gaps in the region	$876,000	29%
Inform Asia	Regional	a) Technical assistance to improve M&E, data quality and use of strategic information; b) Evaluation of malaria elimination models and interventions in Thailand; c) Support on national strategic plans and national M&E plans; d) Local TA for data management in Lao PDR	$524,500	17%
CDC IAA	Regional	Two TDYs for M&E and entomology	$24,500	<1%
USP/PQM	Thailand	Technical assistance to national authorities for ISO accreditation	$50,000	2%
WHO Consolidated Grant	Regional	a) Conduct TES in Thailand, Viet Nam, Lao PDR, and China; b) Support for microscopy training and accreditation in the region and maintenance of regional and national slide banks; b) Maintenance of microscopes; c) Coordinate and facilitate regional training courses	$875,000	29%
USAID	Regional	Staffing and administration costs	$650,000	22%
Total			**$3,000,000**	**100%**

Table 2: Budget Breakdown by Activity

President's Malaria Initiative – *Thailand/Regional*

Planned Malaria Obligations for FY 2016

Proposed Activity	Mechanism	Total Budget (Thailand + Regional)			Thailand	Regional	Geographic Area	Description
		Total $	Commodity $		Total $	Total $		
PREVENTIVE ACTIVITIES								
Insecticide-treated Nets								
LLIN/LLIHN procurement and distribution	TBD - Supply Chain Contract	$615,000	$615,000			$615,000	Regional	Support for ~175,000 LLINs and LLIHNs for focus areas and to fill gaps in the region
Distribution costs	TBD - Supply Chain Contract	$175,000				$175,000	Regional	Distribution costs for LLINs/LLIHNs in the region
Subtotal ITNs		$790,000	$615,000		$0	$790,000		
Indoor Residual Spraying								
Subtotal IRS		$0	$0					
Malaria in Pregnancy								
Subtotal Malaria in Pregnancy		$0	$0					
SUBTOTAL PREVENTIVE		$790,000	$615,000		$0	$790,000		
CASE MANAGEMENT								
Diagnosis and Treatment								
Procurement of RDTs, microscopes, and reagents	TBD - Supply Chain Contract	$50,000	$50,000			$50,000	Regional	Procure ~67,500 RDTs/microscopy supplies to reach migrants and to fill regional gaps and outbreaks

67

Activity	Source / Partner					Location	Notes
Training and accreditation for microscopy	WHO Consolidated Grant / ACTMalaria	$90,000		$90,000		Regional	Support for microscopy training and accreditation in the region and maintenance of regional and national slide banks; maintenance of microscopes
Procurement of antimalarials	TBD - Supply Chain Contract	$36,000	$36,000	$36,000		Regional	Procure ~23,000 ACTs to reach migrants and to fill regional gaps and outbreaks
Subtotal Diagnosis and Treatment		$176,000	$86,000	$176,000	$0		
Pharmaceutical Management							
Drug quality assurance	USP/PQM	$50,000	$50,000	$50,000		Regional	Technical assistance to national authorities for ISO accreditation (completion by 2017 in Thailand)
Subtotal Pharmaceutical Management		$50,000	$0	$50,000	$0		
SUBTOTAL CASE MANAGEMENT		$226,000	$86,000	$176,000	$50,000		
HEALTH SYSTEM STRENGTHENING / CAPACITY BUILDING							
Strengthen NMCP capacity	WHO Consolidated Grant / ACTMalaria	$200,000	$200,000	$200,000		Regional	Coordinate and facilitate regional training courses, including subnational training for microscopy, MMFO
Support for strategic information	Inform Asia	$120,000	$120,000	$120,000		Laos	Local resident technical assistance support for epidemiology in Laos
SUBTOTAL HSS & CAPACITY BUILDING		$320,000	$0	$320,000	$0		
BEHAVIOR CHANGE COMMUNICATION							
SUBTOTAL BCC		$0	$0	$0	$0		

MONITORING AND EVALUATION

Activity	Mechanism	Total	Amount 1	Amount 2	Amount 3	Location	Description
M&E and surveillance strengthening	Inform Asia	$304,500	$200,000	$104,500		Thailand and Regional	Technical assistance to improve M&E, data quality and use of strategic information and evaluation of malaria elimination models and interventions in Thailand and Lao PDR; support will be provided in revising national strategic plans as well as updating national M&E plans
CDC technical assistance for M&E	CDC IAA	$10,000		$10,000		Regional	One CDC TDY
Therapeutic efficacy surveillance network (including K13)	WHO Consolidated Grant	$585,000	$150,000	$435,000		Regional	Conducting TES studies in four countries (Thailand, Laos, Viet Nam, China); technical assistance and monitoring visits by WHO PI to all six GMS countries; support for drug policy review; convening of bi-annual meeting; monitoring of K13 markers
Technical assistance support for TES in Thailand	Inform Asia	$100,000	$100,000			Thailand	Technical assistance support for TES
Technical assistance for entomology	CDC IAA	$14,500	$14,500			Thailand	1 CDC TDY
SUBTOTAL M&E		**$1,014,000**	**$464,500**	**$549,500**	**$0**		

OPERATIONAL RESEARCH

Activity	Mechanism	Total	Amount 1	Amount 2	Amount 3	Location	Description
SUBTOTAL OR		**$0**	**$0**	**$0**	**$0**		

IN-COUNTRY STAFFING AND ADMINISTRATION

Activity	Mechanism	Total	Amount 1	Amount 2	Amount 3	Location	Description
USAID Resident Advisor	USAID	$590,000	$590,000			Regional	Support for USAID Resident Advisor, PMI Malaria FSN Bangkok, administrative costs
Travel costs	USAID	$60,000	$60,000			Regional	Regional travel for RDMA PMI staff

SUBTOTAL IN-COUNTRY STAFFING	$650,000	$0	$0	$650,000
GRAND TOTAL	$3,000,000	$701,000	$514,500	$2,485,500

70

IV. BURMA

(A) Strategy

1. Malaria situation in Burma

Among the six countries of the GMS, the malaria burden is highest in Burma, where it remains a leading cause of morbidity and mortality. Burma has a National Strategic Plan (NSP) for Malaria (2010-2016) that sets malaria prevention and control goals and objectives. The NMCP reported 333,871 malaria cases in 2013, which represents 74.6% of the total malaria cases (447,827) in the GMS. The annual malaria morbidity and mortality rates (see Figure 12) show a decline in cases since 1990.

Figure 11: Malaria morbidity and mortality Rates in Burma between 1976 and 2013 (Source: VBDC)

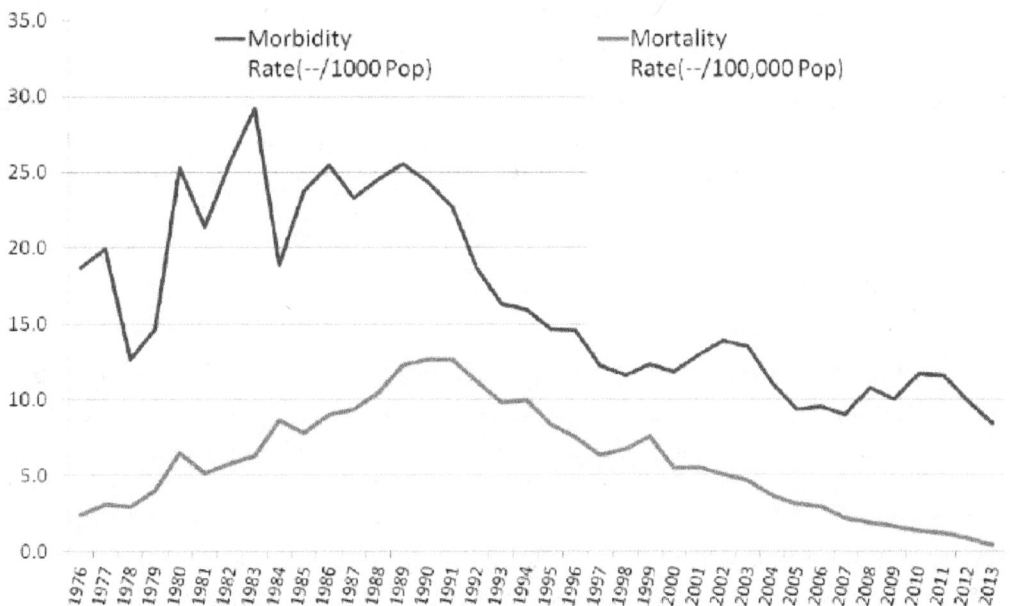

Malaria mortality has declined steadily over the last ten years; and more recently, the NMCP reported the following malaria morbidity figures: 567,452 malaria cases in 2011; 480,586 cases in 2012; and 333,871 in 2013. The total number of hospital inpatient malaria cases has also steadily declined in the last ten years from 62,073 in 2005 to 18,362 in 2013. While the number of reported malaria deaths has progressively fallen in the past two decades from a peak of >5,000 in 1991 to 1,261 in 2007, 788 in 2010, and 236 in 2013, the number of confirmed cases has increased due to scaling up of diagnostics using microscopy and especially RDTs at community levels. Furthermore, the reported data represent only the public sector and are thought to reflect only 25-40% of the total burden. Missing from the data are cases that are self-treated or treated in the private sector, which are estimated to represent more than 50% of the total. Additionally, several malaria-endemic areas, particularly in the Non-State Actor areas and those bordering Thailand and China, are difficult to access by government health services and international organizations. In 2011, WHO estimated the malaria burden in Burma at 1.5 million, by adjusting

71

the 2010 figure for incompleteness of the reporting system, potential over-diagnosis without a parasitological confirmation, and utilization of private sector services.

According to the NSP, 284 townships out of a total 330 townships, are located in malaria-endemic areas and approximately 62% of the population lives in malaria risk areas (21.4% in high-risk, 17.9% in moderate-risk and 22.4% in low-risk areas). Based on 2013 HMIS data, the five states/regions with the highest number of malaria cases are Rakhine (48,247), Sagaing (39,953), Shan (27,870), Kachin (26,770), and Tanintharyi (20,853), which altogether account for 65% of the total cases.

P. falciparum and *P. vivax* are the major species, with occasional reports of *P. malariae* and *P. ovale*. *P. falciparum* accounts for 70-80% of cases with a slight decline in its occurrence over the past decade. Out of 37 species of *Anopheles* recorded throughout the country, ten species have been found to be infected with the malaria parasite and have been classified according to their vector competence as primary vectors (*An. dirus* and *An. minimus)* and secondary vectors (*An. aconitus, An. annularis, An. philippinensis, An. sundaicus, An. culicifacies, An. maculatus*, and to a lesser extent *An. sinensis* and *An. jeyporiensis*). The peak malaria transmission period is generally between July through October for the majority of the country.

Analysis of the age and sex distribution of reported cases in 2011 indicated a modest over-representation of young adults with male cases accounting for 65% of the parasitologically-confirmed cases, reflecting the risk attributed to occupations such as mining, forest-related activities, rubber tapping, construction, etc. Few studies have been conducted in Burma to assess the burden of malaria in pregnancy (MIP) and a wide variation in parasite prevalence has been found in the last decade among women attending antenatal care (ANC) services, ranging from 3% in Tanintharyi Region, to 12.3% in Mon State, 14.7% in East Shan State, and 37% along the Thai-Burma border.

Areas of concern for artemisinin resistance have been identified within Burma through ongoing drug resistance monitoring. In 2009-2010, the early signs of *P. falciparum* resistance to artemisinins characterized by prolonged parasite clearance time were reported in at least three states/regions (Mon, Tanintharyi, and Bago-East); and evidence of suspected artemisinin resistance was reported in Kachin, Kayah, and Kayin states. As an emergency response, a strategic framework to contain artemisinin-resistant *P. falciparum* was developed and endorsed in 2011. Initially supported by the Three Disease Fund (3DF) through December 2012, the MARC Project activities were started in mid-2011.

More recently, a survey[1] conducted in Burma from January 2013 to September 2014 in ten states/regions and along the Thailand and Bangladesh borders found K13 mutations in 371 (39.5%) among 940 malaria patients tested. Additionally, studies[2] based on multi-country analysis of the genetic mutations significantly associated with artemisinin resistance have

---

[1] Spread of artemisinin-resistant *Plasmodium falciparum* in Myanmar (Burma): a cross-sectional survey of the K13 molecular marker. Lancet Infectious Disease, 2015. Published Online, February 20, 2015.
[2] Independent Emergence of Artemisinin Resistance Mutations Among *P.falciparum* in Southeast Asia. The Journal of Infectious Diseases 2015; 211: 670–9

suggested that these mutations originated independently in multiple locations and therefore containment efforts in one area will have limited or no effect on preventing the emergence of resistance in other areas. The strategy has shifted to elimination of *P. falciparum* from the entire GMS.

2. Health system delivery structure and organization

Burma's health system has a pluralistic mix of public and private services. The MOH is taking the responsibility of ensuring comprehensive health care services covering activities for promoting health, preventing diseases, providing effective treatment, and rehabilitation. Some ministries (e.g. Ministry of Defense) also provide limited health care services, mainly curative, for their employees and families. The private, for-profit sector is fragmented in different delivery channels, ranging from traditional healers to General Practitioners, mainly providing ambulatory care, and private clinics, mostly in some large cities. The private, not-for-profit sector is mostly run by community or religious-based organizations supporting institutional care and social health protection.

The MOH structure was recently reorganized in April 2015 into six different departments: Public Health, Medical Care, Medical Research, Health Professional Development and Management, Food and Drug Administration, and Traditional Medicine. Three task forces have been established for financial management, human resources development, and health sector development. Burma aspires to achieve Universal Health Coverage as part of its Vision 2030 for a healthier and more productive population. Malaria control activities are led by the Vector Borne Disease Control (VBDC) program and housed in the newly established Department of Public Health, with the collaboration of partners from public and private sectors. At central level, the VBDC is mandated to formulate national strategies, policies, standards and norms related to malaria control, provide training, conduct operational research, control outbreaks, and provide consultative and advisory services to implementing agencies.

There has been a steady growth in the number of basic health facilities (Table 9) as well as health manpower (Table 10) during the recent past. Of the 29,832 doctors working in 2012-2013, 17,032 were private practitioners and the remainder served in the public sector.

Table 9: Health facilities in Burma (2008-2013)

Health Facilities	2008-09	2009-10	2010-11	2011-12	2012-13
Hospital Public Sector: - Ministry of Health - Other Ministries	820 26	844 27	897 27	921 66	944 66
Total no. of hospital beds	38,249	39,060	43,789	54,503	55,305
Primary & secondary health centers	86	86	86	87	87
Maternal & child health centers	348	348	348	348	348
Rural health centers	1,481	1,504	1,558	1,565	1,635
Traditional medicine hospitals	14	14	14	14	16
Traditional medicine clinics	237	237	237	237	237

Table 10: Health staffing and manpower in Burma (2008-2013)

Health Manpower	2008-09	2009-10	2010-11	2011-12	2012-13
Doctors public sector	9,583	9,728	19,450	11,675	12,800
Doctors private sector	14,157	14,808	15,985	16,402	17,032
TOTAL Doctors	23,740	24,536	26,435	28,077	29,832
Dentists public sector	777	703	756	774	802
Dentists private sector	1,315	1,605	1,806	1,996	2,209
TOTAL dentists	2,092	2,308	2,562	2,770	3,011
Nurses	22,855	24,242	25,644	26,928	28,254
Dental nurses	244	262	287	316	344
Health assistants	1,822	1,845	1,883	1,893	2,013
Lady health visitors	3,238	3,278	3,344	3,371	3,397
Midwifes	18,543	19,051	19,556	20,044	20,617
Health supervisor (1)	529	529	541	612	677
Health supervisor (2)	1,484	1,645	2,080	1,718	1,850
Traditional medicine practitioners: - Public sector - Private sector	950 5,397	890 5,737	890 5,737	885 5,867	875 5,979

Source: Health in Myanmar (Burma), 2013. Web site of Burma's MOH

With rapid development and change, Burma committed to quadrupling its national budget for health, in 2010 the budget allocated to health was only 1% of the total national budget; however, by 2012-2013, it was increased to 3.9%, and in 2014 the domestic health expenditure reached $600 million.

3. National malaria control strategy

In 2014, the NMCP and partners agreed to extend the current National Strategic Plan (NSP) for Malaria Prevention and Control (2010-2015) to 2016 to align the implementation period of the 3MDG and Global Fund grants into its strategy. The goal of the NSP remains the same: to reduce malaria morbidity and mortality by at least 60% by 2016 (baseline: 2007 data), and contribute towards socioeconomic development and the Millennium Development Goals.

The objectives were revised to reflect artemisinin resistance containment initiatives and to address the recommendations made by the external evaluation team in August 2012 and are as follows:

1. By 2016, at least 90% of the people in all malaria risk villages in 284 malaria-endemic townships and 100% of population living in artemisinin resistance containment areas are protected against malaria by using insecticide-treated nets/long-lasting insecticide-treated nets complemented with other appropriate vector control methods, where applicable;

2. By 2016, malaria cases in each township receive quality diagnosis and appropriate treatment in accordance with national guidelines, preferably within 24 hours after appearance of symptoms;
3. By 2016, in 284 malaria-endemic townships, the communities at risk for malaria actively participate in planning and implementing malaria prevention and control interventions;
4. By 2016, the Township Health Department in 284 malaria-endemic townships are capable of planning, implementing, monitoring, and evaluating malaria prevention and control programs with management and technical support from higher levels;
5. To contain artemisinin resistance and eventually eliminate *P. falciparum* malaria in artemisinin resistance affected areas and at the same time prevent, detect quickly, and contain epidemics by targeting mobile and migrant populations;
6. To strengthen the partnership by means of intra- and inter-sectoral cooperation and collaboration with public sector, private sector, local and international non-governmental organization (NGOs), UN agencies, and neighboring countries and promote basic and applied field research.

Implementation of the NSP is guided by epidemiological stratification, which was initially developed in 2007[1], classifying the different areas of the country into malarious (stratum 1), potentially malarious (stratum 2), or non-malarious (stratum 3). Operationally, each malarious area of stratum 1 is further stratified as high-risk (1a), moderate-risk (1b), or low-risk (1c). Using the same stratification criteria based on risk factors, Burma has since conducted micro-stratification exercises in 80 townships in 2007[2] and in an additional 50 townships in 2011[3]. Malaria interventions are prioritized for strata 1 according to this malaria risk stratification. There is a need however to reassess the risk stratification criteria and methodology based on more updated epidemiological information.

Following the principles outlined by the WHO's Global Plan for Artemisinin Resistance Containment (GPARC), the MARC framework was conceived and endorsed in 2011 with the aim of halting the spread of artemisinin resistance from eastern Burma to the western part of the country and beyond. Under this framework, 21 townships were classified as Tier 1 (areas with confirmed resistance), 31 townships as Tier 2 (townships bordering areas with confirmed resistance and with significant inflows of people from Tier 1), and Tier 3 (remainder of the country). Since then, intensive coverage of activities has been initiated in the MARC areas to contain artemisinin resistance including scaling up of community-based diagnosis and treatment, preventive measures including LLINs, and targeted BCC interventions.

4. Strategic updates

- **Restructuring of Ministry of Health.** In early 2015, the Ministry of Health underwent restructuring which created a Department of Medical Services and Department of Public

---

[1] Guidelines on micro-stratification of areas for malaria prevention and control in Myanmar (Burma). 2007
[2] Malaria risk micro-stratification in 80 Townships supported by UNICEF
[3] Malaria risk micro-stratification in 50 Townships, Global Fund, Round 9

Health. The NMCP now falls under the Department of Public Health which oversees activities on communicable diseases, nutrition, school health, environmental health, and other public health initiatives. It is anticipated new staff will be recruited to fill these new positions within the new MOH structure and departments.

- **Updated National Strategic Plan.** In 2014, the NMCP and partners extended the current National Strategic Plan for Malaria Prevention and Control (2010-2015) until 2016 to align the MARC Project and Global Fund efforts and timelines. The objectives of the NSP remain largely the same; however, it now includes some activities to address artemisinin resistance.

- **National Population and Housing Census.** The last national census conducted in Burma was in 1983. Updated information on the country's population became available through a nationwide census conducted in March/April 2014. According to the provisional results, released in August 2014, the total population of the Republic of the Union of Myanmar (Burma) is estimated at 51,419,420. This is a significant reduction from the 60 million that had been estimated prior to this census. It is also important to note that not all areas were enumerated and estimated population figures were used for some townships in Rakhine, Kachin, and Kayin states.

- **Molecular markers for artemisinin resistance.** Studies evaluating the presence of K13 mutants have shown that the predominant K13 mutant found in Myanmar (Burma) does not appear to have spread from Cambodia but likely arose independently. In December 2014, the NMCP revisited the designation of Tiers to respond to the recent evidence of artemisinin resistance. Based on molecular findings, the distribution of the genetic biomarker for artemisinin resistance was more widely distributed than previously thought; however, this evidence alone was not sufficient to suggest confirmed resistance correlated with clinical outcomes. Nonetheless, all 48 townships in Mon, Kayin, Tanintharyi, Kayah and East-Bago states/regions were classified as Tier 1 (confirmed/suspected resistance) and the rest of the country as Tier 2. The Tier 3 category was dropped.

- **Political commitment to malaria elimination.** Burma, together with the other 17 countries attending the 9th East Asia Summit in November 2014, adopted the historical goal of malaria elimination from the entire Asia Pacific region by 2030. This unanimous and enthusiastic commitment of the high-level political leaders represents a strong stimulus for all national malaria programs and the international donor community to further engage resources and scientific attention to this ambitious but technically achievable goal.

5. Integration, collaboration, and coordination

Funding

In recent years, Burma has seen a dramatic increase in both external and domestic funding for health. Following the withdrawal of the Global Fund in Burma in 2005, the 3DF was set up to replace this gap. The 3DF project (2006-2011) provided $25 million for malaria and was one of the first consortia of donors to provide support for malaria control as well as the response to artemisinin resistance through the MARC framework. Since then, Burma has received funding support namely from the following:

- Global Fund: Round 9 ($33 million for malaria for the period 2011-2012), New Funding Model ($74.7 million for malaria for the period 2013-2016), and the Regional Artemisinin Initiative (RAI: $40 million for the period 2014-2016);

- Three Millennium Development Goals (3MDG) Fund is a $300 million initiative primarily focused on strengthening the national health system and improving maternal and child health services, but has also funding allocated for malaria ($16.1 million for the period 2014-2016);

- Funding from DFID and BMGF for the Artemisinin Monotherapy Replacement Project (£11.3 million from DFID, $1 million from Good Ventures, and other funds from BMGF) is implemented by PSI and is working to replace artemisinin monotherapy and other sub-standard antimalarial drugs available in the informal private market sector with subsidized quality-assured ACTs;

- JICA's 10-year project, which has provided funding for health and malaria programs, ended in March 2015 but a new malaria project focusing on elimination in Bago is expected to commence in 2015.

- WHO, DFAT, and the BMGF support for malaria control initiatives and activities.

Table 11. Current funding landscape in Burma

Funding	Total Budget in USD (Funds Disbursed)	Duration	Key Implementing Partners	Key Activities
Domestic*	1,028,807			Staff salaries, trainings, limited quantity of drugs and diagnostics, IEC materials, reporting forms, infrastructure, and operational costs.
GF SSF R9 NFM (Phase II)	74,700,000	2013-2016	NMCP, WHO, MMA, MRCS, MCC, UNOPS (PR) CESVI, HPA, IOM, Merlin, PSI, SCi-M, WVI, SCF (PR)	Prevention, case management, vector control, community mobilization in 284 townships
Three Millennium Development Goal Fund (3MDG)	16,100,000	2014 – 2016	MHAA, MAM, PSI, BI- KMSS, World Concern	Complement the national response on MARC; in line with MARC framework- priority in 52 townships of Tier 1 and 2 as per current zonation
DFID / BMGF / Good Ventures	17,000,000 + 1,000,000	2011 – 2016	PSI	Artemisinin Monotherapy Replacement (AMTR) Project
GF RAI	40,000,000	2014 – 2016	NMCP, MAM, WHO, MMA, Merlin, ARC, PSI, UNOPS (PR)	Prevention, case management, vector control, active case detection, and directly observed therapy, capacity building of health care providers in 52 townships in Tier 1 and Tier 2
JICA*	3,000,000 (TBC)	2015-2016		TA, capacity building, limited quantities of LLINs, drugs, diagnostics, entomology, surveillance, malaria elimination approaches

Sources: World Malaria Report 2014; www.theglobalfund.org; www.gatesfoundation.org; www.Three Diseases Fund.org; www.adb.org; Figures in parentheses are disbursed amounts; *Funding per year

Coordination

The various malaria control initiatives conducted by the NMCP and implemented with the assistance of about 25 different international and national organizations are coordinated through a Technical and Strategic Group (TSG) for malaria. The Malaria TSG comprises technical experts from the MOH, United Nations agencies, national and international NGOs, and donors, including PMI. As the Secretariat for the TSG, WHO organizes periodic meetings for improved coordination and discussion of technical topics on an *ad hoc* basis. There are two sub-working groups (M&E and Program Implementation) that have been recently established under the TSG.

Private Sector

In Burma, PSI supports the "Sun Quality Health Network," a franchise of licensed general practitioners serving low-income populations. As of December 2012, the network included 901 clinics, located in 177 townships, which were providing a range of services, including malaria diagnosis and treatment. As mentioned above, PSI is also implementing the Artemisinin Monotherapy Replacement (AMTR) Project which provides quality-assured ACTs to the private market sector.

Similarly, the Myanmar (Burma) Medical Association (MMA), with support from Global Fund, 3DF, 3MDG, USAID, and WHO, has a network of private general practitioners under its project "Quality Diagnosis and Standard Treatment of Malaria." The private general practitioners are being supported with training and logistics to deliver quality-assured diagnosis and treatment of malaria. Approximately 330 private providers in 113 townships and 360 Village Health Volunteers in 12 fixed and mobile clinics are part of the network.

Growing support for malaria control activities is also provided by the corporate private sector:

- 28 Burmese companies, members of Myanmar (Burma) Health & Development Consortium and Myanmar (Burma) Business Coalition on AIDS, have signed a corporate commitment to provide education on malaria testing, diagnosis, and treatment;
- Total Exploration and Production supports a comprehensive malaria program in 33 villages (population 38,000) surrounding their pipeline in Tanintharyi Region, in addition to collaboration with NGOs on outreach activities;
- Shwe Taung Group ensures health insurance and malaria prevention program to all its 3,304 employees;
- Dagon International provides testing and treatment for 100 permanent staff and 500 seasonal laborers on their palm oil plantation;
- South Dagon and Yuzana provide assistance to health facilities and malaria programs at their plantations in Tanintharyi.

Other USG

PMI is collaborating with USAID/Burma's "Project for Local Empowerment" (PLE) by providing technical assistance in the training of ethnic group volunteers and distributing ACTs, RDTs and LLINs. The PLE Project is funded by USAID for the period 2011-2017 ($8-$10 million per year) and covers six Thai provinces on the Thai-Burma border, including nine Burmese refugee camps.

Another example of USG collaboration is the "Shae Thot Project", which is funded by USAID and implemented by a consortium of international NGOs in the central dry-zone of Burma. This is a comprehensive community development project, which also includes health and malaria control components.

US Peace Corps plans to set up programs in Burma in 2015-2016, and PMI will explore opportunities for collaboration to strengthen malaria control and prevention activities at the community level in Burma.

6. Progress on coverage/impact indicators to date

There have been demographic surveys jointly conducted every five years by the Department of Population and UNFPA since 1991. In the past, Multiple Indicator Cluster Surveys have been jointly conducted by the Ministry of National Planning and Economic Development, the Ministry of Health, and UNICEF. These surveys primarily assessed the situation of women and children and also included data collection on nutrition.

For malaria, more recently there was a baseline household prevalence survey conducted in the MARC areas (Tier 1 and Tier 2) along the Thai-Burma border in 2011-2012. Due to funding and approval delays, this survey was carried out towards the tail-end of the malaria transmission season and noted very low malaria prevalence.

Demographic Health Surveys (DHSs) and Malaria Indicator Surveys (MISs) have never been conducted in Burma, but both surveys have been planned in 2015 and preparation activities are now underway.

Table 12: Evolution of Key Malaria Indicators in Burma from 2012 to 2014

Indicator	2012, Baseline MARC survey	2013 CAP-M survey Tanintharyi, Rakhine, Kayin	2012-2013-2014 Global Fund's Implementing Partners	2013-2014 PMI's CAP-Malaria Project
% Households with at least one bed net	97.4%	82%	2013: 99.3% 2014: 97.2%	
% Households with at least one ITN	35.1%	37.8%	2013: 68%	2013: 97.6% 2014: 97.3%
% Household members who slept under an ITN the previous night	15.9%	20.7%	2013: 86% 2014: 62.7%	2013: 61% 2014:82%
% of Children under five who slept under an ITN the previous night	19.4%		2013: 58.5% 2014: 44.6%	
% Pregnant women who slept under an ITN the previous night	20.3%		2013: 56.5% 2014: 42.4%	
% Children under five years old with fever in the last two weeks for whom advice or treatment was sought			2013: 11.6% 2014: 7.5%	
Test positivity rate			2012: 23.4% 2013: 19.1% 2014: 8.1%	2013: 7.5% 2014: 4.7%

7. Challenges and opportunities

Challenges

- **Coordination among donors and implementing partners.** With increased external international funding coming into the country, there is great potential for improving the health status of the people of Burma. However, one of the main challenges is the lack of coordination amongst donors, implementing partners, and stakeholders. Coverage at township level does not necessarily mean that all villages in the township have access to malaria services and commodities. Micro-stratification and donor mapping exercises have been conducted but never completed at national scale to help inform the coordination of various partners' malaria activities at the village and district levels.

- **Inaccessible areas due to armed conflict.** Despite tremendous progress in expanding coverage of malaria services throughout the country, there are remote areas of the country that still remain inaccessible, particularly in non-state controlled areas, due to security concerns.

- **National general elections:** Burma is planning to hold general elections in late 2015. The period leading up to and after these elections could be particularly tense and could potentially affect program implementation. The general elections could affect the peace process in non-state controlled areas.

- **Future of donor funding**: The Global Fund (RAI and NFM) malaria grants and 3MDG malaria funded activities are scheduled to end in 2016. There has been no information about continued funding for malaria activities by these donors beyond 2016 which presents some challenges for future planning and programming of malaria efforts in-country.

Opportunities

- **Increased domestic investments in health and human resources development.** In recent years, the Government of Burma has made significant commitments and investments in health. With increased international as well as domestic funding in health and infrastructure, Burma has made human resource capacity strengthening one of its priorities. For example, in April 2015, the government nearly doubled the salary of government workers. With the significant increases expected in the public sector workforce, there are opportunities to build the capacity of this cadre of public servants in program management and basic malariology through short courses and professional development training.

- **Electrification and increased telecommunications.** The World Bank has announced a US $2 billion multi-year development program that will dramatically improve access to energy and health care for poor people and support other key government development priorities. With improved mobile telecommunication services in the next two years through contracts with Norway's Telenor and Qatar's Ooredoo, there are opportunities for mHealth initiatives to improve how people access health services and how data are generated and reported.

- **Capacity for operational research.** The Department of Medical Research has been at the forefront of malaria research in the country. While there is substantial in-country capacity to design, implement, and publish operational research activities, there are opportunities to improve linkages with the international community of research institutions and organizations.

- **Commitment to malaria elimination.** Burma, together with the other 17 countries attending the 9th East Asia Summit in November 2014, adopted the historical goal of malaria elimination from the entire Asia Pacific region by 2030. This unanimous and enthusiastic commitment of the high-level political leaders represents a strong stimulus for all national malaria programs and the international donor community to further engage resources and scientific attention to this ambitious but technically achievable goal.

(B) Operational Plan

1. Insecticide-treated nets

NMCP/PMI objectives

According to the 2010-2016 National Strategic Plan for Malaria Control, Burma's NMCP aims to achieve 80% coverage of the population in moderate and high-risk areas using ITNs and LLINs. The NMCP strategy classifies a total of 284 townships as endemic, of which 212 are targeted for scaling up coverage of LLINs/ITNs and retreatment of nets. The strategy has an objective of two LLINs/ITNs per household, provided free, through mass distribution campaigns to the population residing in high- and moderate-risk areas within the 212 townships, with replacement of the LLIN after three years. The strategy defines high-risk groups as populations residing in moderate- and high-risk villages, internal migrant workers (e.g. forest-related activities, mining, agriculture, road and dam construction, etc.) and new settlers in endemic areas.

Progress since PMI was launched

As with other countries in the region, Burma has a "net culture" with a high rate of conventional net use. According to the 2010–2016 National Strategic Plan for Malaria Control, many families in Burma already use mosquito nets, but rates are highly variable and many nets are untreated. A 2008 survey by the Myanmar (Burma) Council of Churches conducted in 160 malaria-endemic and hard-to-reach villages in Chin State, Kachin State and Sagaing Division showed that 91% of households own any type of mosquito net (treated and untreated) with an average of two nets per household. However, coverage of nets treated with insecticide (e.g., ITNs or LLINs) is very low, with only an estimated 5.6% of the total population protected by any ITN. Similarly, the MARC survey (2011-12) found household ownership of nets was 97%, but ITN and LLIN ownership only 35% and 18%, respectively.

Burma's LLIN needs are met primarily through the Global Fund NFM and the RAI grants which cover 14 of the 17 states and regions, with most of the targeted townships in the eastern and southern part of the country. In 2011 and 2012, 1.3 million LLINs were distributed and 2.5 million conventional nets retreated using all sources of support, including the Global Fund. In 2013, the Global Fund, JICA, 3MDG, and PMI contributed 1.9 million LLINs. In 2014, Global Fund partners reported distributing over 376,000 LLINs. With FY 2013 funds, PMI procured and distributed approximately 326,456 LLINs through implementing partners targeting populations residing in its targeted areas, hard-to-reach populations (residing in non-state areas), and migrant and mobile populations.

Progress during last 12-18 months

PMI procured 553,500 LLINs with FY 2014 funding for distribution in focus areas and expanded project areas (up to 27 townships) to help address urgent needs and protect vulnerable populations. A small quantity of these LLINs are provided to private sector employers as an approach to reach temporary and seasonal migrant populations working on plantations, agriculture production and construction projects in focus areas.

With FY 2014 funds, PMI will begin an assessment of LLIN survivorship, attrition, physical durability, and insecticidal activity in project areas, coordinating closely with the NMCP on data monitoring and collection. This assessment is especially important for LLIN need projections as the current NSP is based on replacement after three years. Evidence from a number of PMI focus countries in Africa indicates that significant numbers of LLINs do not remain effective for the projected three- to five-year time frame.

Commodity gap analysis

Table 13: LLIN Gap Analysis for Burma

Calendar Year	2015	2016	2017
Total targeted population*	26,800,000	27,070,680	27,344,094
Continuous Distribution Needs			
Estimated Total Need for Continuous	-	-	-
Mass Distribution Needs			
*Estimated Total Need for Campaigns***	8,211,382	4,892,849	1,502,130
Total ITN Need	**8,211,382**	**4,892,849**	**1,502,130**
Partner Contributions			
ITNs from Global Fund (UNOPS PR)	1,100,489	1,901,490	-
ITNs from Global Fund (Save the Children PR)	324,922	104,300	-
ITNs from Global Fund RAI UNOPS PR	1,190,000	1,236,826	-
ITNs planned with PMI funding	853,500	300,000	456,000
Total ITNs Available	**3,468,911**	**3,542,616**	**456,000**
Total ITN Surplus (Gap)	**(4,742,471)**	**(1,350,233)**	**(1,046,130)**

Note: Global Fund malaria grants will end in 2016; therefore no estimates are available for LLINs planned in 2017 from Global Fund-supported partners.

* Risk population is calculated based on the population estimate from UNOPS using the recent population census conducted in 2014. At-risk population includes Strata 1a, 1b, and 1c; Annual population growth rate (1.01%)

** Total distribution need calculated as (population at risk / 1.8)-# of nets previously distributed to target areas. Assumes resulting gap will need to be met the following year. Target Areas covers 284 townships in strata 1a, 1b, and 1c (Global Fund targets 1a and 1b; PMI targets strata 1a, 1b, and 1c in focus states/regions - Rhakine, Thanitharyi, Bago, and Kayin).

Plans and justification

Although Burma has funding from the various donors in specific focus areas, there remain gaps in LLIN coverage in the country. PMI will procure approximately 456,000 LLINs and hammock nets in FY 2016 to fill LLIN gaps at the household level in endemic areas, targeting villages and townships in the cross-border focus areas and those that are not supported under the current Global Fund agreement (e.g., southern Rakhine townships, non-state areas), including reaching migrant and mobile populations with LLINs. PMI estimates LLINs based on prior year's consumption and the quantities distributed by implementing partners who are working with marginalized populations mainly through workplace and outreach distribution channels. In addition, PMI will continue to monitor LLIN survivorship, attrition, and physical integrity monitoring in project areas.

Proposed activities with FY 2016 funding: ($2,050,000)

- **Procurement and distribution of ITNs (LLINs and LLIHNs):** PMI will procure approximately 456,000 LLINs and hammock nets to fill LLIN gaps at the household level in endemic areas, targeting villages and townships in the PMI implementation areas and those that are not supported under the current Global Fund agreement (e.g., southern Rakhine townships, non-state areas, potential expansion to new areas), including reaching migrant and mobile populations with LLINs. ($1,500,000)

- **Community-level support for distribution, promotion, and use of ITNs:** PMI will support distribution and delivery of LLINs through mass distribution to reach households and migrant populations, BCC to promote use of LLINs and treated material/ hammock nets through trained village malaria volunteers. PMI will target ITN distribution to townships in project areas depending on existing gaps and PMI resources. ($450,000)

- **Net Durability Assessment:** PMI will continue to support the assessment of LLIN survivorship, attrition, physical integrity and insecticidal activity monitoring in project areas. The assessment will follow the basic PMI Guidance for Routine Monitoring of LLINs, with modifications to meet the specific needs of Burma. ($100,000)

2. Malaria in pregnancy

NMCP/PMI objectives

PMI supports a two-pronged approach to reduce the burden of malaria infection among pregnant women including provision of LLINs and effective case management of malaria and anemia, especially amongst the most vulnerable populations including migrant workers, refugees, and other hard-to-reach populations. Because of the low prevalence of malaria, IPTp is not part of any national strategy in the GMS, including Burma. The NMCP strategy supports free distribution of LLINs to all households in areas of high and moderate risk; however, there is no national policy for provision of LLINs to pregnant women attending antenatal care (ANC) services. According to the 2011-12 MARC survey conducted in the Tier 1 areas, the percentage of households with at least one ITN in Burma is 35% and LLIN use among pregnant women is 20%. ANC attendance is generally high in all GMS countries. In Burma, most pregnant women attend ANC at least once (80%) and most pregnant women complete the recommended four visits (73%).

Burma's national malaria treatment policies for pregnant women follow WHO recommendations: quinine is used in the first trimester (which may be combined with clindamycin) and ACTs in the second and third trimester (as stated in the national strategic plan). Treatment for severe malaria is with IV or IM artesunate.

Data on the burden of malaria in pregnancy in the region is limited. A 2002 review of 17 studies on malaria during pregnancy in Burma reported a low prevalence of clinically-suspected malaria among pregnant women (1-2% of total outpatient and inpatient burden). A separate 2005 study found that 11% of pregnant women attending antenatal care and 12% of all women delivering in Eastern Shan State and Mon State were infected with malaria. The states and divisions reporting the highest incidence are Rakhine, Kachin, and Kayah. Wide variations in prevalence of malaria parasitemia in women attending ANC services were reported, ranging from 3% in Tanintharyi Division to 37% elsewhere along the Thai-Burma border, where the majority of women were asymptomatic and infected with *P. falciparum*. The role of female migrants may also be underestimated in the region; small studies conducted by PMI partners in Burma found more than 50% of migrants in their catchment areas are women.

Progress since PMI was launched

With FY 2013 funding, PMI assisted the NMCP to update its policies especially for areas of confirmed artemisinin resistance, ensuring integration of malaria in pregnancy guidelines across relevant national programs (e.g. Maternal Health Program).

Progress during last 12-18 months

With FY 2014 funding, PMI supported the development of a malaria module which addresses MIP as part of the national training for auxiliary midwives. PMI is also supporting the development of ethnically appropriate BCC materials and messages directed to the prevention and early treatment-seeking for suspected cases of malaria in pregnancy for use by village malaria volunteers at the community level and nurse midwives at Rural Health Units.

In addition, in FY 2014, a PMI implementing partner screened over 5,000 pregnant women attending ANC services and found only three malaria-positive cases. It found a similarly low percentage of malaria-positive cases (0.07%) during the first two quarters of FY 2015 with more than 4,000 pregnant women screened at ANC. However, when the same partner screened over 116,000 people in the same period through its mobile malaria outreach and community mobilization activities in targeted project areas as well as remote villages, it found a 6.6% malaria-positive rate among pregnant women (total tested was 759 of which 50 were positive for malaria) as compared to 2.2% malaria positivity rate among non-pregnant women of reproductive age (15-49 years, total women tested was 26,063 of which 585 were positive for malaria). Based on these findings, the partner concluded that screening through routine ANC is not an appropriate approach for detecting malaria infection among pregnant women but improved case finding and management by VMWs and enhanced surveillance by mobile outreach teams are needed.

Plans and justification

PMI will continue to support malaria in pregnancy activities in Burma to ensure that malaria and maternal health programs implement coordinated strategies and their guidelines, supervision and training activities are consistent. In addition, PMI will assess malaria treatment-seeking practices and barriers to seeking antenatal care through a qualitative assessment among women of child-bearing age (including pregnant women) in malaria-endemic villages. An exploration of this issue will be conducted for women in both stable and migrant populations and will focus on differential malaria burden among pregnant women who do and do not seek care through ANC services.

Proposed activities with FY 2016 funding: ($50,000)

- **Assessment of treatment-seeking practices among women of reproductive age at risk for malaria:** PMI will continue to support malaria in pregnancy activities in Burma to improve coordination between malaria and maternal health programs. PMI will also support a qualitative assessment to identify treatment-seeking practices and barriers to seeking antenatal care and explore additional factors for higher malaria prevalence noted in the community to ensure that pregnant women among both stable and migrant populations have access to malaria services at Rural Health Units. ($50,000)

- **Strengthen case management of malaria in pregnancy:** Support for training of facility health workers and VMWs in malaria diagnosis and treatment, including specific guidance on the treatment of malaria during pregnancy. (see Case Management section)

3. Case management

Diagnosis and treatment

<u>NMCP/PMI objectives</u>

The national malaria treatment policy, which was developed in 2002, was first updated in February 2008 with further revisions and updates provided in 2011, 2014, and 2015. Three ACTs (artemether-lumefantrine (AL), DHA-Pip or artesunate-mefloquine (A+M)) are currently recommended for the treatment of *P. falciparum* cases along with a single dose of primaquine prescribed on Day 0 without a prior G6PD deficiency test. Artemisinin monotherapy use in both formal and informal sectors is strictly prohibited and has been banned. Adherence to the national malaria treatment policy among health care providers is not uniform in part due to approximately 60-70% of suspected malaria patients receiving treatment from the private sector. Treatment for *P. vivax* is chloroquine and primaquine for radical cure; however, there is a reluctance to use primaquine especially in the private sector, as well as poor adherence to the 14-day regimen. For severe malaria, parenteral artesunate is recommended. In addition, Burma is piloting directly observed therapy (DOT) and enhanced follow up to determine the proportion of patients with persistent parasitemia on Day 3.

The national diagnostic policy is confirmatory testing with either microscopy or a combination RDT before treatment for malaria is prescribed. In hospitals and higher-level health facilities, microscopy is the preferred diagnostic method. RDTs are being scaled up in lower-level facilities and at the community level through VHWs and VMWs. Microscopy availability is limited primarily to townships. Records indicate that presently there are about 1,000 malaria microscopy centers nationwide, 330 of them located in township hospital laboratories: however, it is estimated that only about 60% are fully functional and their quality needs further strengthening. Burma's NMCP is one of the biggest users of RDTs in the GMS and distributed 958,925 RDTs in 2013.

Although diagnosis and treatment of malaria is free in the public sector, the majority of persons with malaria seek treatment from private sector providers, where diagnostic testing may not be available or may be of poor quality. Private sector sales account for the majority of malaria treatments provided in Burma. DFID and other donors have supported the subsidized ACT treatment project that has been successful in removing artemisinin monotherapy from many retail outlets. Rapid replacement of oral artemisinin monotherapy with quality-assured ACTs, Supa Arte, has occurred in the informal private sector with 1 million courses of subsidized ACTs sold from January to October 2014.

Progress since PMI was launched

PMI has invested in improving diagnostic capacity through strengthening microscopy services as well as equipping and training community-level volunteers to utilize RDTs for parasitological confirmation. A diagnostic quality assurance system was updated in 2009, with training and technical support provided by WHO and ACTMalaria, but the quality of current microscopy testing is still inadequate.

Since the launch of PMI, 600,875 RDTs and 64,674 ACTs have been procured and distributed. PMI began supporting community-level malaria case management in 2011 in seven townships in Tanintharyi and Kayin and has expanded to 26 townships to include Rakhine and Kayah states. To date, 1,247 village volunteers have been trained in malaria case management, including diagnostic testing, in focus townships in Tanintharyi, Kayin, and southern Rakhine. These VHWs have performed 27,694 RDTs on patients with suspected malaria and treated 1,869 confirmed cases (862 *P. falciparum*, 948 *P. vivax*, 59 mixed) with antimalarials.

In non-state actor areas, Back Pack Health Worker Teams (BPHWT) have promoted increased access to health services for vulnerable populations in South East Burma, with support from the Project for Local Empowerment (PLE) project. Through mobile health teams, BPHWT provides primary health care including malaria diagnosis with RDTs and treatment with ACTs and community health education and prevention for internally-displaced persons and other vulnerable populations in conflict-affected and rural areas of Burma.

In the private sector, PSI's "Sun Quality Health Network" (SQHN) Project operates a private sector social franchise of clinics and shops which has now scaled-up to 863 SQHN general practitioners and over 2,057 Sun Primary Health (SPH) providers within PSI's Sun network providing malaria diagnosis and treatment services at 193 and 87 townships, respectively. In 2014, PSI distributed ~400,000 RDTs and 35,000 ACTs through the Sun Network. In total, 325,034 suspected malaria cases were tested with RDTs and 15,571 were treated with ACTs.

PMI has strengthened and expanded private sector case management to target townships in Chin, Magway, Shan (S), and Kayah states.

Progress during the last 12-18 months

With FY 2014 and 2015 funding, PMI will procure 270,000 RDTs and 24,540 ACTs. With FY 2014 funding, 1,887 health care providers (1,054 VMWs, 736 health staff, and 97 laboratory technicians) have been trained on malaria diagnosis and 1,790 health care providers (1,054 VMWs and 736 health staff) have been trained on case management in 26 townships. These health care providers have performed 160,904 RDTs on patients with suspected malaria and treated 7,423 positive cases (4,013 *P. falciparum*, 3,013 *P. vivax*, 312 mixed) with antimalarials. PMI has provided 18,400 RDTs and 3,220 ACTs along with 18,400 LLINs to the BPHWT along with malaria case management training to reach internally-displaced persons and other hard-to-reach populations in the non-state areas. In total, 13,417 suspected malaria cases were tested and 2,308 cases were treated with ACTs.

In the private sector, PMI is strengthening and expanding private sector case management from 11 townships in Chin, Magway, Shan (S), and Kayah States to 16 townships in Chin, Magway, Shan (N), Shan (E), Shan (S), Sagaing, Kayah, and Kachin. Over the past 18 months, 25 doctors and 320 VHWs have been trained in malaria diagnosis and treatment through the SPH network. They have tested approximately 10,800 fever cases using RDTs and treated 1,836 confirmed malaria cases.

PMI has also supported a regional workshop on quality assurance of malaria microscopy. The most recent external competency assessment in Burma occurred in 2012. PMI is conducting an external assessment of National QA/QC policies, including updating standard operating procedures to be in line with current WHO recommendations, and updating training curriculum for training and re-training. A national slide bank, as well as a core group of expert microscopists (as trainers and/or validators), are being established. With FY 2014 funding, 128 health facility staff have been trained on microscopy.

PMI's support for therapeutic efficacy studies in Burma are described below in the "Surveillance: Drug resistance and therapeutic efficacy studies" section. Briefly, DHA-Pip efficacy testing for *P. falciparum* at four and artemether-lumefantrine testing at three sites in 2014 showed ACPR >90%. Three sites completed chloroquine efficacy testing in 2014 against *P. vivax* which also showed high ACPR >90%.

Commodity gap analysis

Table 14: RDT Gap Analysis

Calendar Year	2015	2016	2017
RDT Needs			
Target population at risk for malaria*	26,800,000	27,068,000	27,344,094
Total number projected fever cases (suspected malaria)**	2,601,112	2,627,383	2,653,920
Percent of fever cases confirmed with microscopy**	0.084	0.084	0.084
Percent of fever cases confirmed with RDT**	0.974	0.974	0.974
Total RDT Needs	**2,533,483**	**2,558,818**	**2,584,406**
Partner Contributions			
RDTs carried over from previous year	-	-	471,808
RDTs from Global Fund (UNOPS)	1,360,722	2,413,987	-
RDTs from Global Fund (Save the Children)	235,825	182,684	-
RDTs from 3 MDG	7,660	133,955	-
RDTs planned with PMI funding	300,000	300,000	270,000
Total RDTs Available	**1,904,207**	**3,030,626**	**741,808**
Total RDT Surplus (Gap)	**(629,276)**	**471,808**	**(1,842,598)**

Note: Global Fund and 3MDG malaria funding ends in 2016 and there is uncertainty about Global Fund allocations post-2016; therefore estimates of planned RDTs in 2017 are not available.
* Risk population is calculated based on the population estimate from UNOPS using the recent population census conducted in 2014. This risk population includes the population from stratum 1a, 1b, and 1c; assuming annual population growth rate at 1.01%.
** Estimates from World Malaria Report, 2014 (excluding private sector estimates); assuming annual population growth at 1.01%.

Table 15: ACT Gap Analysis

Calendar Year	2015	2016	2017
ACT Needs			
Target population at risk for malaria*	26,800,000	27,070,680	27,344,094
Total projected number of malaria cases**	201,926	161,541	129,233
Total ACT Needs*	**252,408**	**201,926**	**161,541**
Partner Contributions			
ACTs carried over from previous year	-	26,828	89,186
ACTs from Global Fund (UNOPS)	201,316	191,564	-
ACTs from Global Fund (Save the Children)	11,100	7,980	-
ACTs from 3 MDG	26,820	24,740	-
ACTs planned with PMI funding	40,000	40,000	20,000
Total ACTs Available	**279,236**	**291,112**	**109,186**
Total ACT Surplus (Gap)	**26,828**	**89,186**	**(52,355)**

Note: Global Fund and 3MDG malaria funding ends in 2016; therefore estimates of planned ACTs in 2017 are not available. Global Fund allocations are uncertain post-2016.
* Risk population is calculated based on the population estimate from UNOPS using the recent population census conducted in 2014. This risk population includes the population from stratum 1a, 1b, and 1c; assuming annual population growth rate at 1.01%.
** Estimated from World Malaria Report, 2014; assuming 20% reduction annually
*** Estimated need includes buffer, distribution inefficiencies, increasing coverage, and shifting of care-seeking from the private sector to the public sector

Plans and justification

Ensuring the availability of quality-assured diagnostics and antimalarials is critical in PMI programming. PMI will continue supporting scale-up of diagnostic testing and treatment at community and primary care levels, in the private sector, and in non-state areas through the provision of commodities, refresher training of existing laboratory staff and health workers in the performance and use of malaria microscopy and RDTs, case management, and strengthening quality assurance systems in PMI focus areas.

Based on available consumption data from prior years of implementation and currently reported overstock of RDTs and ACTs at the national level due to over-estimation of malaria burden, PMI will scale down the procurement of RDTs and antimalarials, but will remain vigilant and ready to fill critical gaps when supply chain or financial lapses impede their availability. As the malaria burden will eventually decline in many parts of Burma, PMI will assess feasible ways of integrating delivery of malaria services at community and health facility levels.

Proposed activities with FY 2016 funding: ($4,131,000)

- **Procure RDTs and microscopy supplies.** PMI will procure approximately 270,000 RDTs and microscopy supplies for focus areas and non-state areas for use by community level health volunteers or workers. ($200,000)

- **Procure antimalarials:** PMI will procure approximately 20,000 ACTs and other antimalarials for use by community level health volunteers or workers in focus and non-state areas. ($30,000)

- **Support strengthening national diagnostics QA/QC system:** Following the assessment of the national diagnostic policies and EQA, the standard operating procedures and training curriculum will be updated. PMI will provide technical assistance and training of key staff to strengthen the national reference laboratory as well as support development of a slide bank. ($100,000)

- **Private sector quality assurance:** PMI will continue to strengthen diagnosis and case management among private providers identified in focus areas as well improve data reporting from the private sector. ($300,000)

- **Training and supervision of diagnostics and case management at facility and community levels in PMI focus areas:** Training and supervision of malaria case management through community health workers, rural health center staff, and auxiliary midwives, including delivery of integrated case management where appropriate. ($3,501,000)

Pharmaceutical management

NMCP/PMI objectives

Ensuring the availability and use of antimalarial medicines, diagnostics and preventive commodities is a high priority for the NMCP and PMI. As the revised national malaria strategic plan sets the objective on strengthening and expanding case management in the public sector, the importance of the logistics management and continuous availability of malaria commodities becomes more emphasized.

Health commodities are procured and distributed in Burma in two ways: through the VBDC; and the Central Medical Store Depot (CMSD). The VBDC distributes laboratory supplies and antimalarial drugs to township hospitals and health departments throughout Burma. Additionally, it supplies sub-national VBDC teams located in states and divisions. Township health departments then are responsible for the distribution to the station hospitals, rural health centers, and sub-rural health centers. The second system managed by the CMSD is within the Medical Care Services of the Department of Health. The CMSD purchases antimalarial drugs using government funds in consultation with the VBDC. The CMSD distributes to all township hospitals and health departments. Since 2002, UNICEF has supported Supply System Management Officers whose duty it is to strengthen the supply and logistics systems within the MOH. The USAID Mission is currently supporting a strategic review and assessment of the national supply chain system with the MOH and working at the national level to develop strategies for improved coordination among the NMCP, Supply Chain Management Systems, donor agencies, NGOs and UN agencies on commodities management and logistics, but specifically focusing on HIV/AIDS products. PMI will coordinate with Mission's efforts while focusing on strengthening systems for malaria commodities. Coordination of commodities management among donors and partners is a critical area of support that is needed in Burma due to potential vertical programs and projects.

The Global Fund grants (NFM and RAI) cover procurement and distribution of ACTs, RDTs, and other malaria medicines for the 284 malaria-endemic townships. VBDC provides malaria services in all 284 townships with support from other partners. Procurement for ACTs and other malaria medicines under the Global Fund is handled by the two Principal Recipients (Save the Children and United Nations Office for Project Services (UNOPS)) for their sub-recipients. Initially, the 3MDG Fund imported malaria commodities on behalf of implementing partners; however, it scaled down this activity when Global Fund expanded its support for malaria commodities.

Progress since PMI was launched

PMI support for pharmaceutical management and commodities to Burma primarily consists of monitoring availability of commodities (medicines, diagnostics, and LLINs) supplied through the

Global Fund; facilitating procurement and distribution of PMI-funded commodities to fill gaps not addressed by the Global Fund grant; and providing targeted technical assistance, micro-planning, and/or logistics support as needed to support full coverage of malaria interventions in the focus areas of Tanintharyi Division, Kayin, and Rakhine states.

Progress during the last 12-18 months

In FY 2014, following a national quantification exercise, the NMCP identified a large gap in moderate-risk areas (strata 1b) under the Global Fund NFM. Approximately 553,000 LLINs would be needed for 47 townships. In response, PMI was able to procure these LLINs and assisted with the micro-planning and distribution plans. PMI recruited a supply chain consultant to assist with the lengthy importation process, coordination with NMCP, UNOPS, and other stakeholders for storage and coordination with freight forwarders in-country.

PMI also has been coordinating with the Supply Chain Management System and other supply chain partners in Burma through quarterly logistics management information system (LMIS) harmonization workshops to ensure standardization of forms and reporting. In addition, PMI participates in the quarterly partner's meetings on supply chain forecasting and planning exercises with NMCP, UNOPS, WHO, and other stakeholders.

Plans and justification

To ensure availability of key commodities in PMI implementation areas as well as to respond to urgent requests from other areas, PMI will monitor and address potential bottlenecks in procurement and distribution of malaria commodities (including Global Fund-financed commodities). As with any transition period, there is potential for significant commodity gaps when the Global Fund's NFM and RAI come to an end in 2016. PMI will monitor the situation closely and will be prepared to mobilize commodities as needed. Special attention will be paid to support community-level logistics to target cross-border migrants through the development of simple inventory tools, storage and transport boxes, etc. Due to the relatively nascent supply chain system in Burma, PMI will support a local technical advisor to work closely with the NMCP, MOH, and other stakeholders to address these critical supply chain issues.

Proposed activities with FY 2016 funding: ($200,000)

- **Support for pharmaceutical management and logistics:** Technical assistance (based in Rangoon) in supply chain management will be provided to Burma's MOH to strengthen coordination for malaria commodities (including pharmaceutical management systems, forecasting, quantification, management, and distribution of pharmaceuticals and RDTs). ($200,000)

Drug quality

NMCP/PMI objectives

Given the large quantities and varieties of antimalarials available in the private sector and the high malaria burden in the country, Burma is felt to be vulnerable to the introduction and sale of counterfeit and substandard antimalarial drugs and artemisinin monotherapies. In 2009, WHO and USP found that most of the staff that had been trained to conduct drug quality testing were no longer present, nor were there adequate equipment and reagents. In addition, the national reference laboratory at the Food and Drug Administration (FDA) had only one high performance liquid chromatography machine and one refurbished dissolution machine; and it had no standards for registration of malaria medicines. The assessment also found that there was a severe need for equipment, supplies, and training at the national reference laboratory.

One of the specific objectives of the National Malaria Strategic Plan is to address counterfeit or substandard drugs and ban oral artemisinin based monotherapy. The FDA is a key player in fulfilling this objective. The FDA takes responsibility in monitoring drug quality, banning monotherapy as well as upgrading its quality assurance laboratory and capacity building of inspectors. As FDA has stopped registration and renewal of any licenses of artemisinin monotherapy, all existing licenses of artemisinin monotherapy have expired on December 2012. Furthermore, with support from the DFID-funded Artemisinin Monotherapy Replacement (AMTR) project, the availability of artemisinin monotherapies has significantly reduced and appears to have been withdrawn/phased out from markets. The FDA will reinforce its regulatory action to ensure monitoring for artesunate monotherapy as well as substandard and counterfeit antimalarials.

Recently announced, the FDA will strengthen its efforts to protect the country from substandard imported food, medicines and cosmetics, and will also improve the standards of locally produced goods. The FDA currently has offices in Nay Pyi Taw, Yangon and Mandalay with six other branch offices. With the increase in budget and staff, the FDA plans to establish branch offices in 14 districts and to set up laboratories at 14 more border trade zones over the next three years. Moreover, FDA procured high-level drug quality testing equipment for central-level laboratory and Minilabs® for the state/regional offices.

Similar to the vision of the FDA, PMI has a focus on monitoring quality of antimalarial drugs in Burma. When PMI expanded its commitment to Mekong countries in 2011, PMI supported monitoring the quality of antimalarial drugs and building country capacity to curtail the availability of sub-standard or counterfeit drugs. In support of the NSP, PMI works closely with the NMCP, FDA, and other key stakeholders to implement this effectively.

Progress since PMI was launched

PMI is supporting efforts in Burma to collect information on the country's medicine QA/QC systems that are intended to ensure quality of antimalarial medications passing through the public and private supply chain. Sentinel survey protocols were developed and trainings were held on the use of the Minilabs® for field-based testing of medicines collected from a wide variety of venues. Additional staff from the national FDA laboratories in Nay Pyi Taw and Mandalay were trained on compendia testing methods so that they could conduct confirmatory testing of medicines suspected of being falsified. PMI has supported efforts to build capacity in-country through training and provision of technical assistance and has supported the establishment of five sentinel sites for drug quality testing. In addition, PMI has procured essential equipment including a dissolution tester, a high performance liquid chromatography system, and other necessary laboratory and personal safety supplies for use by the FDA laboratories.

Progress during the last 12-18 months

In collaboration with the NMCP, Department of Food and Drug Administration, and Department of Medical Research – Lower Myanmar (Burma), PMI supported a baseline survey on the Quality, Presence, and Source of Priority Antimalarial Medicines in Select Geographical Areas of Burma. Ten out of the 45 antimalarials sampled (mostly chloroquine, quinine, and artemether) failed or were inconclusive.

Plans and justification

PMI will work to ensure that national pharmaceutical reference laboratories are able to conduct the necessary laboratory analyses for post-marketing surveillance of drug quality, both for the timely and accurate analyses of samples from the medicines quality monitoring as well as samples collected through other investigations. Focus will be placed on providing technical assistance to the FDA to reach ISO accreditation.

Due to methodological difficulties with adequate sampling, lengthy confirmatory testing, and limited enforcement capacity, the usefulness of PMI-supported post-marketing surveillance for counterfeit and substandard antimalarials may be limited.

Proposed activities with FY 2016 funding: ($200,000)

- **Drug quality assurance:** Technical assistance will be provided to the FDA to conduct tests on antimalarials and other drugs sampled. Particular attention will be placed on strengthening national quality control laboratories to meet international standards of practices, to attain ISO 17025 accreditation by 2017, and to maintain the certification status. ($200,000)

4. Health system strengthening and capacity building

NMCP/PMI objectives

The National Strategic Plan for malaria control in 2010- 2016 revised its objectives to reflect artemisinin resistance containment initiatives. These objectives intend to improve the key components of malaria control which will ultimately strengthen the overall country's health system.

The strategy focuses on rebuilding the NMCP's health workforce with different skill sets to improve management at various levels of field operations. Additionally, it aims to improve health staff capacity in 284 malaria-endemic townships on planning, implementation, monitoring and evaluation of malaria control activities. These efforts will be supplemented with a strengthened health management information system, evidence-based planning, research and policy development, and increasing access to malaria commodities such as LLINs, quality drugs and diagnostics.

The Government of Burma recently created a Department of Public Health under the Ministry of Health which will require an increased public health workforce with additional skills over the coming years.

Progress since PMI was launched

The NMCP has taken a leadership role in improving key components of the health system with the collaborative support of development partners. As part of the effort to improve the technical capability and quality of health services, the NMCP has set up a series of trainings on malaria prevention, case management, commodities management, program planning and development, and community mobilization. Over the years, the NMCP has trained its key staff at different levels including basic health staff, microscopists, and health care personnel from hospitals, general practitioners and volunteers with the financial and technical support of UNICEF, JICA and WHO. Later, these efforts were scaled up with the support of PMI, 3DF, 3MDG Fund and the Global Fund. PMI collaborates closely with NMCP leadership to achieve the goals of stronger health workforce, strengthened quality health services, reliable health information and continuous availability of essential medical product.

The progress on strengthening the malaria surveillance system is underway. The NMCP has standardized case report forms and made an effort in improving data collection at all levels. Systematic data collection and data transmission have been reinforced over the year through training of NMCP staff as well as basic health staff and provision of computers. Additionally, PMI and the NMCP have assessed the country's surveillance situation in 2013 and subsequently, a plan was drafted to improve the malaria surveillance system and to continue to work with key partners to generate quality, comprehensive data.

Since PMI became fully operational in 2012, it has supported NMCP staff to receive training on specific technical areas such as field epidemiology, malaria field operations management, quality assurance for laboratory diagnostic services, and drug quality testing.

Progress during the last 12-18 months

PMI support of the International Field Epidemiology Training Program (IFETP) for NMCP staff started with FY 2013 funding and has been continued. Currently two NMCP staff are undergoing the final year of IFETP and one staff joined in 2014. In FY 2014, PMI provided technical assistance to the Department of Health on the development of an in-country six-month FETP training course to support long-term capacity building, which will benefit different levels of field staff and strengthen capacity on data collection and epidemiological analysis. PMI has been providing the technical assistance for the curriculum development and other related processes. Planning is underway and training will start in late 2015.

PMI-supported routine monitoring of antimalarial drug efficacy has served as a platform for strengthening in-country research capacity. The NMCP has updated the "National Malaria Treatment Guideline" based on the results of PMI-supported routine monitoring of antimalarial drug efficacy from sentinel sites. Moreover, the information gathered from this drug efficacy study contributed in prioritizing resources for effective malaria interventions.

Plans and justification

PMI will continue to support two fellows to participate in the two-year, full-time, postgraduate competency-based training program, IFETP, which focuses on technical skills in the collection, analysis, and interpretation of data for decision-making and epidemiologic investigations. In addition to the international fellowship, PMI will continue supporting the building of in-country epidemiology capacity of different levels of NMCP staff who are overseeing malaria control activities in the field. With the Ministry of Health restructuring its organizational setup and planning to recruit more public health personnel, continued capacity building around technical skill and knowledge capacity is essential. In order to build more malaria management and field operations capacity, PMI will adapt the regional malaria management field operations (MMFO) course to the local needs and develop an in-country course.

Proposed activities with FY 2016 funding: ($270,000)

- **International Field Epidemiology Training Program (IFETP):** PMI will support two Burmese fellows to participate in the IFETP in Bangkok, Thailand. ($150,000)

- **In-country FETP:** PMI will support building epidemiology and surveillance capacity for state and regional level NMCP staff through participation in a six-month in-country FETP course. ($50,000)

- **Technical assistance for in-country FETP:** PMI will provide technical assistance through CDC TDYs for the curriculum development and on-site support for the in-country FETP. ($20,000)

- **In-country MMFO course:** The regional MMFO training course coordinated by ACTMalaria will be adapted for mid-level managers from selected regions/states and townships. It will focus on malaria program management skills and basic malariology. ($50,000)

Table 16: Summary of health systems strengthening activities cross referenced from other technical areas

HSS Building Block	Technical Area	Description of Activity
Health Services	Case Management, Behavior Change	PMI supports training and supervision of malaria case management to improve malaria services provided by VMWs, community health workers, rural health center staff, and auxiliary midwives. PMI has supported the

	Communication	development of standard operating procedures on quality assurance of diagnostics and will continue to support the implementation these procedures as well as field practices, training and accreditation of malaria microscopists, and establishment of a national slide bank. PMI is also supporting health systems strengthening by expanding coverage and availability of malaria commodities, and creating demand for services through community health education, BCC, and VMW networks in hard-to-reach areas and to reach at-risk, vulnerable mobile/migrant populations.
Health Workforce	Health Systems, Capacity Building	The Ministry of Health has recently created a Department of Public Health, where the NMCP is housed, to provide focused leadership and technical guidance on public health activities in the country. PMI will support the Ministry of Health in building the capacity of its technical staff and health workforce on program management and development. This includes support of two-year long-term international fellowships and a six-month in-country short course on field epidemiology for key NMCP central- and field-level staff. The training will help improve epidemiology skills and capacities at different levels of program management staff for malaria control. PMI will also support the development of an in-country malaria managers field operations training course adapted from the regional course for mid-level managers from selected regions/states and townships.
Health Information	Monitoring & Evaluation, Surveillance, Operational Research	PMI supports strengthening the health information management system through strengthening the malaria surveillance system. PMI will provide technical assistance to the NMCP and supporting surveillance systems at all levels (public, private, community). The implementation plan will include scaling up an electronic database system; supporting NMCP capacity for data management and use; and supporting national M&E plan development. These processes will enable the NMCP to transition its implementation from malaria control to elimination in the future. PMI is also contributing towards building in-country research capacity through routine monitoring of the efficacy of antimalarial drugs in 11 sentinel sites. PMI contributed to information about personal protection measures with a study to evaluate the acceptability and feasibility of using insecticide-treated clothing in Mon State.

Essential Medical Products, Vaccines, and Technologies	Pharmaceutical Management & Logistics, Case Management	PMI will provide technical assistance in supply chain management to the NMCP and strengthen coordination of malaria commodities (including pharmaceutical management system, forecasting, quantification, management and distribution of pharmaceuticals and RDTs). PMI is also strengthening the national quality control laboratories for malaria in order to improve the quality of health services and build the capacity of health laboratory workforce.
Leadership and Governance	Health Systems Strengthening, Capacity Building	PMI will continue to support the coordination among NMCP and development partners to harmonize the strategic efforts in responding artemisinin resistance in Burma, including participation and technical support for the malaria Technical Steering Group and its technical workstreams. PMI's technical assistance to the NMCP will closely align with national strategies and national responses.

5. Behavior change communication

NMCP/PMI objectives

The NMCP, in collaboration with WHO and in consultation with agencies working in malaria control, previously developed a "Communication and Social Mobilization for Malaria Prevention and Control in Burma." This document has served as the framework for BCC activities since 2007. More recently, the NMCP Strategy (2010-2016) recognized the need to update this malaria communication and social mobilization plan to include a budget, human resource requirements, and implementation strategies.

Burma's National Strategic Plan places priority on educating and raising awareness of the target population for malaria prevention and control. With the availability of LLINs, RDTs, and ACTs at the health facility and community levels, BCC and social mobilization activities are relied on to motivate targeted at-risk populations to access and utilize these interventions. VMWs support interpersonal communications on prevention and promotion activities as well as treatment compliance counseling at the community level (one VMW per village). Special high-risk populations targeted with BCC messages include local forest dweller residents, new settlers, internal and external migrant workers, and people crossing national border areas. Key behaviors to influence include use of treated nets, prompt diagnosis and treatment of fever, adherence to treatments, and avoidance of monotherapies and counterfeit drugs. One of the challenges for BCC activities is the more than 135 ethnic groups speaking more than 100 languages and dialects, traditional beliefs related to causes of and remedies for malaria, and mobility of key target groups. A formal BCC workgroup has not yet been established at the national level; however, BCC efforts are discussed in the TSG, within the Program Implementation working group.

The WHO *Strategic Framework for Artemisinin Resistance Containment in Myanmar (Burma) 2011-2015*, identifies BCC as an integral part of all malaria interventions, serving to improve the utilization of available health services offering quality diagnostics and ACTs, reducing the demand for artemisinin monotherapies in the private sector, and improving adherence to the three-day ACT regimen. BCC activities implemented through PMI partners are aligned with the national strategy, and support efforts from national, township to community levels.

Progress since PMI was launched

PMI supports BCC efforts through 1,161 VMWs based in 26 townships in Tanintharyi, Kayin, and southern Rakhine regions. PMI's implementing partners conducted advocacy meetings to sensitize the health and administrative officials from state, township, and village levels on the malaria situation and project plans.

In Kayin state, local Karen ethnic groups benefitted from established community-based malaria interventions and community health worker networks that are integrated within the existing local health structure. These Community Health Groups support the work of trained VMWs. Besides administering RDTs and case management, the VMWs have been trained on community mobilization strategies, education sessions and use of communication tools.

In Tanintharyi Division, the populations included local residents as well as large and small groups of internal migrants working in agricultural plantations and at the Dawei Deep Seaport Project. Mobile malaria education and clinic teams also conduct outreach malaria prevention campaigns with screening of febrile patients for treatment. PMI partners also work with private sector employers to strengthen and improve their malaria services and promote awareness among their temporary and seasonal migrant workers.

PMI has supported the training of 1,161 VMWs in effective case management of malaria and conducting BCC sessions. In 2013, VMWs facilitated health education sessions in interpersonal communication settings and at community mobilization events such as World Malaria Day and approximately 320,000 people received the messages on malaria prevention.

Progress during last 12-18 months

With FY 2014 funding, PMI reached 284,220 people, including 25,636 migrants and mobile populations, with BCC messages and interpersonal communication provided by trained VMWs, mobile malaria teams, and private providers. In addition, PMI partners distributed 186,839 pamphlets and 1,329 posters with malaria prevention and control messages. PMI also collaborated with WHO on a BCC assessment conducted in three countries (Burma, Cambodia, and Thailand) to better understand progress to date and identify remaining gaps to strengthening BCC efforts. The assessment reviewed national BCC strategies and guidelines; the quality and availability of BCC training and materials; existing approaches, messages, tools and job aids being disseminated and utilized on the ground by different projects, and the extent to which the target mobile/migrant populations and local residents are being reached. The report, which will be available in the summer of 2015, will provide recommendations on how BCC and social mobilization activities can be strengthened, delivered more effectively, and messages harmonized within and among the three countries, and country-specific recommendations are expected.

Plans and justification

PMI supports the NMCP strategy of aiming to have at least one VHW per village in all malaria-endemic villages in Burma. Emphasis will be given to interpersonal and group communication comprising up to 70% of BCC efforts. Support will include training and disseminating of already developed BCC materials on malaria prevention, accurate diagnosis, and prompt and effective treatment. The costs of the distribution and LLIN promotion include BCC activities to augment malaria prevention efforts implemented by community health/malaria volunteers in the focus areas and engaging community members and networks, including employers of migrant and forest workers. PMI also supports routine LLIN monitoring post-distribution by village health workers to reinforce BCC messages on LLIN use. Furthermore, PMI will plan to support the NMCP in updating its national BCC strategy.

Proposed activities with FY 2016 funding: ($300,000)

- **BCC for malaria control and prevention interventions**: PMI will support continued efforts to standardize, harmonize, and disseminate key BCC materials and messages at the community level and strengthen interpersonal communication approaches with VMWs and private providers. Also, based on findings from the BCC assessment, PMI will support development and implementation of effective BCC approaches, as well as support the NMCP to update its national BCC strategy. Careful consideration will be given to special and high-risk target groups with BCC approaches focused on improving coverage and use of malaria prevention measures (LLINs and LLIHNs), and increasing awareness of malaria in pregnancy, dangers of counterfeit drugs, as well as prompt diagnosis and effective treatment. ($300,000)

6. Monitoring and evaluation

NMCP/PMI objectives

Burma's National Strategic Plan (NSP) for Malaria Prevention and Control 2010-2016 aims to reduce malaria morbidity and mortality by 60% by 2016 and contribute towards socio-economic development and the Millennium Development Goals. The National M&E plan focuses on collecting 20 indicators through both routine reporting and periodic surveys. These indicators are consistent with PMI indicators. The current public sector malaria information system involves basic health staff submitting monthly reports to their respective Township Health Department which then forwards the report to the State/Regional VBDC Office. The State/Regional VBDC Team then analyzes the data on a quarterly basis and sends feedback to the township level. This system is paper-based and there are major challenges with data flow and analysis. Furthermore, the current system does not effectively or routinely capture information from the private sector or NGOs. Burma conducted a sub-national malaria survey in 2011-2012 in containment zones 1 and

2 as part of the MARC project, but there has not been a national malaria survey that includes coverage estimates and malaria biomarkers.

Malaria is endemic in 284 townships out of 330 townships (high-risk: 21%, moderate-risk: 18%, low-risk: 23%, risk-free: 38%); however, this malaria risk stratification is considered to be outdated. Over the last 20 years, malaria morbidity and mortality rates have progressively decreased reaching 8 confirmed cases per 1,000 population and 0.8 deaths per 100,000 population. Despite the overall trend of reduction of malaria burden, the disease still affects a significant proportion of the country with some remote areas continuing to have high transmission. With PMI support, efforts to strengthen malaria control in areas with evidence of artemisinin resistance have been targeted to cross-border focus areas of Tanintharyi Division, Kayin State, and southern Rakhine. PMI is also strengthening the data collection in these areas through the routine national surveillance systems.

Table 16: Monitoring and Evaluation (surveys conducted or planned in Burma)

Data Source	Survey Activities	Year								
		2009	2010	2011	2012	2013	2014	2015	2016	2017
Household surveys	Demographic Health Survey (DHS)							X*		
	Multiple Indicator Cluster Survey (MICS)	X								
	Malaria Indicator Survey (MIS)				X* (sub-national MARC)			X		(X)
	National Household Census						X*			
	ACTWatch Baseline Survey (Household)					X				
Health Facility and Other Surveys	Health facility survey				X* (sub-national MARC)					
	ACTWatch Baseline (Outlet)					X*				
Malaria Surveillance and Routine System Support	Support to malaria surveillance system					X	X	X	X	X
	Support to HMIS*					X	X	X	X	X
Therapeutic Efficacy Monitoring	In vivo efficacy testing	X	X	X	X	X	X	X	X	X
Entomology	Entomological surveillance and resistance monitoring				X	X	X	X	X	X

*Not PMI-funded

101

Progress since PMI was launched

The first national census in 20 years was completed in April 2014; it has provided the sampling frame for the upcoming Demographic Health Survey (DHS). The first DHS in Burma is planned for mid- 2015 with USAID support. The DHS will provide key indicators for population, health, and nutrition, and will serve to help identify the critical needs in health for the country as well as a nationally representative baseline to measure and monitor progress. The planned DHS will be conducted during the dry season and will not collect malaria biomarkers. However, input has been provided to adapt the standard malaria module to the Burmese context. In collaboration with 3MDG, PMI will contribute to a national Malaria Indicator Survey (MIS) during the peak transmission period using FY 2014 funding. The MIS will include collection of biomarkers for malaria prevalence estimates at national and sub-national levels. Data collection for the MIS will be conducted during the peak transmission season between July and September 2015. The MIS will also serve as a comparison to the MARC malaria survey conducted in 2012 which covered only Tier 1 and Tier 2 areas along the Thai-Burma border but was conducted past the transmission season due to funding delay issues. Designs and plans for the MIS are being closely coordinated in country with the national program and other partners with an MIS Steering Committee chaired by the Director General of the Department of Public Health to provide overall oversight and monitoring. It is anticipated that a follow-up MIS will be conducted two years later in 2017 to allow proper monitoring of outcomes and impact.

Following the surveillance system assessment in Burma funded by PMI in FY 2013, an implementation plan in consultation with the NMCP has been developed. A four-pronged approach of both short- and long-term goals included: 1) Improving the management, processing and analysis of malaria data through implementation of an Access database to replace the current system of Excel spreadsheets; 2) Improving the IT infrastructure in the NMCP by ensuring appropriate network at NMCP and associated IT infrastructure and staff capacity at all levels to manage, secure and share data; 3) Harmonizing VHV reporting systems to maximize data quality, coverage and completeness through standardized volunteer reporting systems, standard operating procedures and an accurate list of all volunteers within the NMCP; and 4) Using mHealth approaches to develop appropriate mechanisms to detect and respond to malaria cases in real-time using a suite of mHealth tools that can be deployed to detect and respond to malaria cases in real-time and respond to emergency stockouts of key commodities.

Progress during the last 12-18 months

In the past year, PMI has invested in an assessment of the national surveillance system leading to the development of an implementation plan and is currently working with other donors, e.g. 3MDG and JICA to ensure that stakeholders are coordinated and supporting a common surveillance system platform in Burma. PMI has supported work to transition away from Excel spreadsheets towards an ACCESS database at the central level. A database manager is now in place in Nay Pyi Taw to support the NMCP on data management and analysis.

Furthermore, PMI is supporting a pilot of the District Health Information System (DHIS-2) in two townships with information reported from village level. This will provide a basis for eventual transition to a more comprehensive nationwide surveillance system as Internet connectivity becomes more widely available. It will allow management and mapping of village-level malaria data and reduce the need for data manipulation at the higher levels. Additionally, this will empower townships to more easily analyze and use their data and to prioritize interventions.

M&E coordination at the national level is managed through an M&E Working Group under the Technical Strategic Group (TSG). Due to staffing turnover at the Secretariat (WHO), the TSG has not been convening regularly; however, the M&E Working Group has convened *ad hoc* meetings. Both PMI staff and implementing partners are active members.

The National Strategic Plan has recently been revised extending the period through 2016, and the National M&E Plan will also be updated. PMI will continue to support and contribute to the development of the National M&E Plan.

Plans and justification

Malaria M&E and surveillance systems in Burma remain fragmented, particularly between implementing partners and the national program. A comprehensive and responsive surveillance system will be critical as the NMCP continues to scale up activities across the country and moves towards the long-term goal of case-based reporting, case investigation, and response.

PMI, in collaboration with other stakeholders, will continue to support strengthening of M&E and surveillance systems in Burma, particularly integration of malaria data from NGOs and the private sector, into one comprehensive national Malaria Information System. As described earlier (see Case Management section), PMI has supported the expansion of the Sun Quality Health Network of private sector clinics and shops to provide quality malaria diagnosis and treatment services. PMI will emphasize integration of data reporting and use from these private sector clinics and shops with the national surveillance system.

Proposed activities with FY 2016 funding: ($700,000)

- **Support for M&E activities and surveillance strengthening**: Technical assistance will be provided to strengthen routine surveillance systems at township, state/region, and national levels towards a comprehensive, integrated system that includes data from public, private, and community sectors. PMI will support the scaling up of electronic database systems as well as NMCP's capacity for data management and use, including technical assistance provided to the NMCP at Nay Pyi Taw. PMI will continue to support the National M&E Plan development and assist in the identification of NMCP M&E needs to move from control to elimination. ($300,000)

- **Surveillance, Monitoring and Evaluation in PMI focus areas:** PMI will require a robust M&E system to monitor progress in the PMI focus areas. This will include focus on piloting and implementing improved data collection systems, data quality audits, and use of strategic information in the PMI target areas to inform areas for program improvement. ($400,000)

7. Surveillance: Drug resistance and therapeutic efficacy studies

NMCP/PMI objectives

The USAID/PMI-supported network for drug efficacy monitoring has been instrumental in the detection of emerging resistance to antimalarial medicines, including artemisinins in 2008. Along with other non-PMI-supported TES sites (e.g., supported through the Global Fund), the TES network has since expanded from 35 to 48 sentinel sites throughout the GMS – of which eight are PMI-supported in Burma.

Progress since PMI was launched

In Burma, PMI currently supports eight sentinel sites on a rotating basis with approximately half of the sites reporting results every two years. Cure rates with an ACPR ranging from 93.8% to 100% were seen in all TES sites against *P. falciparum* with artemether-lumefantrine (AL), DHA-Pip and artesunate-mefloquine (A+M) in the last six years, as summarized in the following Table 17. With the recent discovery that mutations of the Kelch-13 gene act as a causal determinant of delayed parasite clearance, TES provides a platform for the correlation of the clinical outcomes of the current first-line treatments with the prevalence of molecular markers of artemisinin resistance.

Progress during the last 12-18 months

Ongoing TES sites in Burma are assessing the efficacy of DHA-Pip, A+M, and AL for the treatment of uncomplicated *P. falciparum* infections and of CQ for the treatment of *P. vivax* infections in six study sites as well as monitoring for Day 3 positivity rates. More recent results showed acceptable ACPR rates of DHA-Pip AL and AS+MEF against *P. falciparum* and CQ against *P. vivax*. However, in Loikaw, Kayah State, there was a high rate of Day 3 parasitemia to AL (13.7%) and to AS+MEF (25%). Three sites are currently conducting DHA-Pip efficacy testing against *P. falciparum*.

Plans and justification

The TES network to monitor antimalarial drug resistance has been instrumental in assisting national programs to update their national treatment policies and guidelines. PMI plans to continue support of therapeutic monitoring in Burma using standardized WHO protocols, including screening for K13 mutations in TES sites.

Proposed activities with FY 2016 funding: ($220,000)

- **TES network:** Support for in-country designated TES sites including K13 monitoring, technical assistance from WHO investigator, monitoring, and biannual TES meetings. ($220,000)

8. Surveillance: Entomology

NMCP/PMI objectives

As rapid ecologic changes occur with economic development, deforestation, and scale-up of LLINs in Burma, there is an urgent need to collect up-to-date, standardized data. The forested areas and possibly some plantations in the GMS are home to the region's most efficient malaria vector, *An. dirus*, with secondary vectors, *An. minimus* and *An. maculatus*, found in the forest and forest-fringe areas and possibly in the new orchard and rubber plantation ecologies. JICA has been the main partner supporting the NMCP in entomologic capacity building and PMI is coordinating closely with JICA on its entomological support. JICA has also recently announcement the design of a new malaria project following the conclusion of their previous five-year project to address infectious diseases (HIV, TB, and Malaria) in Burma. The new project will include support for entomologic research for malaria elimination.

Progress since PMI was launched

PMI is currently supporting entomological surveillance in nine study villages in four townships. The project plan[1] is for one collection every two months; two entomological survey trips have already been made, with three to four collection nights per site. Each study involves four collectors: two indoors for a 12-hour collection period and two outdoors for a six-hour period. Despite its importance as a vector in Burma, *Anopheles dirus s.l.* was not collected in high densities in any of the study sites. Limited insecticide susceptibility tests conducted indicate pyrethroid susceptibility in *Anopheles annularis* and *An. jamesi*, but further insecticide resistance monitoring is necessary to evaluate resistance in malaria vector populations in this area.

Progress during the last 12-18 months

In FY 2014, a two-week entomology workshop jointly organized by JICA and PMI was conducted and trained 45 participants from the NMCP in vector surveillance and control. Two additional five-day workshops were conducted for 15 NMCP entomologists and assistant entomologists focusing on hands-on training in testing procedures to identify, monitor and manage the resistance to insecticide among malaria vector mosquitoes, insecticide susceptibility testing, and sporozoite detection by ELISA. More recently an information-sharing session on malaria entomology was conducted in Rangoon for partners working on entomology.

In consultation with the NMCP, JICA, and other stakeholders, a medium-term capacity development plan for public health entomology and vector control was developed early this year. This plan reviewed the current policies for entomology and vector control, identified training needs and gaps, and potential partnerships and coordination for the next five years.

---

[1] Moh Seng Chang, Report on Entomological Project Review – USAID/CAP-M (May 2013)

Plans and justification

PMI continues to support regional strengthening of entomologic surveillance, insecticide resistance monitoring, and development and evaluation of methods to interrupt outdoor transmission. PMI continues to engage with the JICA to strengthen entomologic capacity in the region. The two highest priorities for PMI are development of a strategic plan for entomology and LLIN durability monitoring. PMI's planned investments in entomologic surveillance, trainings, technical support, and procurement of supplies will be in support of the comprehensive entomologic plan for Burma.

Proposed activities with FY 2016 funding: ($129,000)

- **Support for entomologic surveillance (basic package):** PMI will continue to support entomological monitoring in the target townships and the insectary in Rangoon. In these focus areas, basic entomological testing will occur at sentinel sites in collaboration with JICA and VBDC. ($90,000)

- **Technical support for entomological studies and training.** Two CDC TDYs by an entomologist will be provided to build capacity and provide technical assistance on entomological studies and durability monitoring of LLINs. ($29,000)

- **Procurement of supplies:** Expendable supplies and reagents for entomologic surveillance at sentinel sites in Burma, as well as supplies for the insectary in Rangoon. ($10,000)

9. Operational research

NMCP/PMI objectives

The recently revised NSP 2010-2016 highlighted the following key issues for the Malaria Technical and Strategy Group (TSG) to develop a research agenda:
1. Development and validation of tools and delivery mechanisms for effective prevention and case management of malaria among migrant workers/ forest-related workers, ethnic groups, and pregnant women.
2. Drug resistance monitoring (including *P. vivax*)
3. Effective strategies for eliminating fake and counterfeit medicines
4. Mosquito behavior change, insecticide resistance, risk of importation of vectors
5. Studies on alternative vector control that reduces reliance on insecticides
6. Assessment of novel tools such as suppositories, *P. vivax* rapid tests, insecticide-treated hammock nets
7. Economics of inter-sectoral action for malaria prevention and control, e.g. in plantations and coastal areas.

Specific operational research topics included in the NSP included ways to improve motivation and the quality of health staff, evaluation of "standby treatment" used for forest-related workers and other mobile groups, and research focusing on elimination of resistant *falciparum* malaria (e.g., the significance of Day 3 parasitemia).

Progress since PMI was launched

Along with other development partners, PMI has procured a significant number of LLINs in Burma. However, personal protection against outdoor transmission has not been adequately addressed by the national program. PMI has focused its operational research support thus far on evaluating additional personal protection measures to address outdoor transmission e.g. the occupational use of insecticide-treated clothing.

Progress during the last 12-18 months

Over the past 12 months, a PMI-funded study to evaluate the acceptability and feasibility of using insecticide-treated clothing amongst rubber tappers in Mon State was conducted. Preliminary findings suggest acceptability of insecticide-treated clothing was very high with no significant difference between the insecticide-treated and non-treated clothing arms. Ninety four percent of respondents in both arms reported liking the clothing overall, and perceived the clothing to reduce mosquito bites (92.1%), to provide warmth (91.6%), to be pleasant to wear for nighttime work (95.6%), to be easy to clean (92.1%), and to be comfortable (93.8%). Further analyses with funding from DFID will investigate acceptability during the upcoming rainy season and assess residual insecticidal activity following routine use.

Table 17: PMI-funded Operational Research Studies

Completed OR Studies			
Title	**Start date**	**End date**	**Budget**
N/A	N/A	N/A	N/A
Ongoing OR Studies	**Start date**	**End date**	**Budget**
Title			
Preference and acceptability of permethrin insecticide-treated clothing in Mon State	February 2015	September 2015	$127,500
Planned OR Studies			
Title	**Start date**	**End date**	**Budget**
N/A	N/A	N/A	N/A

Plans and justification

PMI will support operational research as key programmatic questions arise.

Proposed activities with FY 2016 funding: ($0)

There are no proposed OR activities in FY 2016.

10. Staffing and administration

One health professional serves as the Resident Advisor to oversee PMI in Burma, representing USAID. In addition, one FSN works as part of the PMI team. All PMI staff members are part of a single inter-agency team led by the USAID Mission Director or his/her designee in country. The PMI team shares responsibility for development and implementation of PMI strategies and work plans, coordination with national authorities, managing collaborating agencies and supervising day-to-day activities. Candidates for resident advisor positions (whether initial hires or replacements) will be evaluated and/or interviewed jointly by USAID and CDC, and both agencies will be involved in hiring decisions, with the final decision made by the individual agency.

The PMI professional staff work together to oversee all technical and administrative aspects of PMI, including finalizing details of the project design, implementing malaria prevention and treatment activities, monitoring and evaluation of outcomes and impact, reporting of results, and providing guidance to PMI partners.

The PMI lead in country is the USAID Mission Director. The PMI resident advisor, from USAID, reports to the Senior USAID Health Officer for day-to-day leadership. The technical expertise housed in Atlanta and Washington guides PMI programmatic efforts and thus overall technical guidance for the RA falls to the PMI staff in Bangkok, Atlanta, and Washington.

The PMI resident advisor is based within the USAID health office and is expected to spend approximately half their time sitting with and providing technical assistance to the national malaria control programs and partners.

Locally hired staff to support PMI activities either in Ministries or in USAID will be approved by the USAID Mission Director. Because of the need to adhere to specific country policies and USAID accounting regulations, any transfer of PMI funds directly to Ministries or host governments will need to be approved by the USAID Mission Director and Controller, in addition to the USG Global Malaria Coordinator.

Proposed activities with FY 2016 funding: ($750,000)

- Support for USAID/PMI Resident Advisor (including 100% FSN and in-country support, administrative costs). ($700,000)

- Travel cost support for RDMA staff. ($50,000)

Table 1: Budget Breakdown by Mechanism

President's Malaria Initiative - *Burma*

Planned Malaria Obligations for FY 2016

Mechanism	Geographic Area	Activity	Budget ($)	%
TBD	Target areas	a) Community case management including implementation, training, and supervision; b) Support for diagnosis and case management in the private sector; c) BCC for malaria control and prevention interventions; d) Surveillance and M&E strengthening, including project M&E; e) Support for entomological surveillance	$5,491,000	61%
TBD - Supply Chain Contract	Target areas	a) LLIN/LLIHN, RDTs and ACT procurement; b) Strengthening the pharmaceutical management systems	$1,930,000	21%
CDC IAA	National	a) FETP support for two Burmese fellows; b) Entomologic surveillance supplies; c) TAs for LLIN durability, M&E, entomology	$259,000	3%
WHO Consolidated Grant	National	a) Conduct TES studies; b) Strengthen in country epidemiology and management capacity; c) Support strengthening national/subnational QA/QC for malaria diagnosis	$370,000	4%
USP-PQM	National	a) Drug quality assurance; b) Technical assistance and strengthening national quality control laboratories	$200,000	2%
USAID	National	Staffing and administrative costs	$750,000	8%
Total			**$9,000,000**	**100%**

Table 2: Budget Breakdown by Activity

President's Malaria Initiative - *Burma*

Planned Malaria Obligations for FY 2016

Proposed Activity	Mechanism	Budget Total $	Budget Commodity $	Geographic Area	Description
PREVENTIVE ACTIVITIES					
Insecticide-treated Nets					
Procurement of ITNs	TBD - Supply Chain Contract	$1,500,000	$1,500,000	Target areas	Procure 456,000 LLIN/LLIHNs for focus areas and non-state areas including migrants and mobile populations
Distribution of ITNs	TBD	$450,000		Target areas	LLIN distribution, promotion and BCC in focus areas. Distribution will target stable populations and special populations including migrants and pregnant women
LLIN durability monitoring	TBD	$100,000		Sentinel sites	Routine monitoring (Year 3 of durability assessment)
Subtotal ITNs		$2,050,000	$1,500,000		
Indoor Residual Spraying					
Subtotal IRS		$0	$0		
Malaria in Pregnancy					
Assessment of treatment-seeking practices among reproductive age women at risk for malaria	TBD	$50,000			Qualitative assessment to identify treatment-seeking practices and barriers to seeking antenatal care and explore higher malaria prevalence in the community ensuring pregnant women among stable and migrant populations have access to malaria services

Activity	Funding source	Cost	Cost	Area	Description
Strengthen case management of malaria in pregnancy	TBD				See Case Management section
Subtotal Malaria in Pregnancy		$50,000	$0		
SUBTOTAL PREVENTIVE		$2,100,000	$1,500,000		
CASE MANAGEMENT					
Diagnosis and Treatment					
Procurement of RDTs/microscopy supplies	TBD - Supply Chain Contract	$200,000	$200,000	Target areas	Procure 270,000 RDTs/ microscopy supplies for focus areas and non-state areas for use by community level health volunteers or workers
Procurement of antimalarials	TBD - Supply Chain Contract	$30,000	$30,000	Target areas	Procure 20,000 ACTs + other antimalarials for use by community level health volunteers or workers in focus and non-state areas
Support strengthening national/subnational QA/QC for malaria diagnosis	WHO Consolidated Grant / ACTMalaria	$100,000		Nationwide	Training and accreditation of microscopists
Support to diagnosis and case management in the private sector	TBD	$300,000		Target areas	Support diagnosis and case management among private providers identified in focus areas
Case management at the community level, including implementation, training, and supervision	TBD	$3,501,000		Target areas	Training and supervision of malaria case management through community health workers, rural health center staff, and auxiliary midwives, including integrated case management where appropriate
Subtotal Diagnosis and Treatment		$4,131,000	$230,000		
Pharmaceutical Management					
Support for supply chain management	TBD - Supply Chain Contract	$200,000		Nationwide	Technical assistance in supply chain management to Burma MOH and strengthen coordination on malaria commodities (including pharmaceutical management system, forecasting,

111

Activity	Funding Source	Budget	Subtotal	Location	Description
					quantification, management and distribution of pharmaceuticals and RDTs).
Drug quality assurance	USP/PQM	$200,000		Nationwide	Technical assistance and strengthening national quality control laboratories
Subtotal Pharmaceutical Management		$400,000	$0		
SUBTOTAL CASE MANAGEMENT		$4,531,000	$230,000		
HEALTH SYSTEM STRENGTHENING / CAPACITY BUILDING					
Field Epidemiology Training Program (FETP)	CDC IAA	$150,000		Nationwide	Support two Burmese fellows to participate in international FETP in Bangkok
In-country FETP	CDC IAA	$50,000		Nationwide	Conduct in-country FETP short-course training
Technical assistance for in-country FETP	CDC IAA	$20,000		Nationwide	Two technical assistance TDYs for in-country FETP training
In country malaria management field operations (MMFO) course	WHO Consolidated Grant / ACTMalaria	$50,000		Nationwide	Strengthen in country epidemiology and management capacity
SUBTOTAL HSS & CAPACITY BUILDING		$270,000	$0		
BEHAVIOR CHANGE COMMUNICATION					
BCC for malaria control and prevention interventions	TBD	$300,000		Target areas	Support to standardize, harmonize and disseminate key BCC materials and messages at the community level and strengthening interpersonal communication approaches with VMWs and private providers; technical support for updating national BCC strategy
SUBTOTAL BCC		$300,000	$0		
MONITORING AND EVALUATION					

Activity	Funding Source		Amount	Location	Description
Surveillance and M&E strengthening	TBD		$300,000	Nationwide	Strengthening routine surveillance systems at all levels (public, private, community), including scaling up of electronic database systems; support NMCP capacity for data management and use, including TA in NPT; support national M&E plan development; support NMCP M&E needs to move from control to elimination
Monitoring and evaluation in PMI target areas	TBD		$400,000	Target areas	Strengthen surveillance, monitoring and evaluation; improve data collection systems, data quality, and use at township and state levels in PMI target areas
Therapeutic Efficacy Surveillance	WHO Consolidated Grant		$220,000	Sentinel sites	Conducting TES studies at 10 sites in Burma, including technical assistance and drug policy review
Entomological surveillance (basic package)	TBD		$90,000	Sentinel sites	Support for entomological monitoring; insectary support in Rangoon (in collaboration with JICA/VBDC)
Technical assistance for entomology	CDC IAA		$29,000	Sentinel sites	Two TDYs for entomologic support
Entomologic surveillance supplies	CDC IAA		$10,000	Sentinel sites	Reagents and supplies
SUBTOTAL M&E			**$1,049,000**		
OPERATIONAL RESEARCH		$0	$0		
SUBTOTAL OR		$0	$0		
IN-COUNTRY STAFFING AND ADMINISTRATION					
USAID	USAID		$700,000		USAID Malaria advisor, 100% Malaria FSN Burma, in-country and regional travel, administrative costs
RDMA technical assistance	USAID		$50,000		Technical assistance and TDY support from RDMA PMI staff

SUBTOTAL IN-COUNTRY STAFFING	$750,000	$0	
GRAND TOTAL	**$9,000,000**	**$1,730,000**	

114

V.   CAMBODIA

(A) Strategy

1.   Malaria situation in Cambodia

Over the last decade, many of Cambodia's key health indicators have improved as the country's economy has developed. Malaria nevertheless remains a major contributor to the public health and economic burden in Cambodia, with a reported incidence in the public sector of 4.3 cases per 1,000 population in 2011. Eighty percent of the population lives in areas without malaria transmission, but around 20% (approximately 2.9 million people) either live permanently in the forested endemic areas or are "forest dependent" for additional income. The 2010 Cambodia National Malaria Survey estimated a malaria prevalence of 0.9% in high-risk areas (<2km from the forest).

Figure 12: Trend of reported malaria confirmed cases in Cambodia (2009-2015*) (Source: CNM)

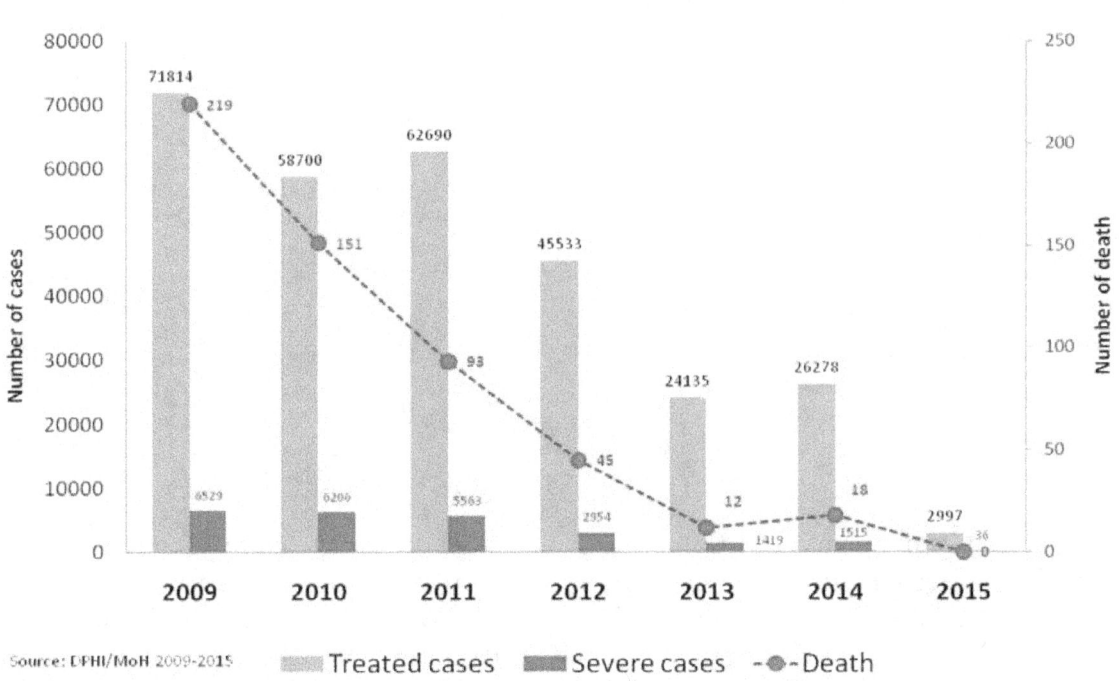

Source: DFHI/MoH 2009-2015   Treated cases   Severe cases   -●-Death

* Data available through Q1 (2015)

115

Both malaria morbidity and mortality rates have declined over the last decade due to an increased government commitment and substantial financial and technical support from the international community. Prevalence of *Plasmodium* infection by microscopy has declined in each successive national survey since 2004. Weighted national prevalence by microscopy was 4.4% in 2004, 2.6% in 2007, 0.9% in 2010 and 0.1% in 2013. In addition, the health information system (HIS) and VMW malaria data for 2012 indicated a reversal of the *P. falciparum:P. vivax* ratio--further evidence of the recent effectiveness of Cambodia's national malaria control efforts.

Figure 13: Annual parasite index in Cambodia, by OD (Source: CNM)

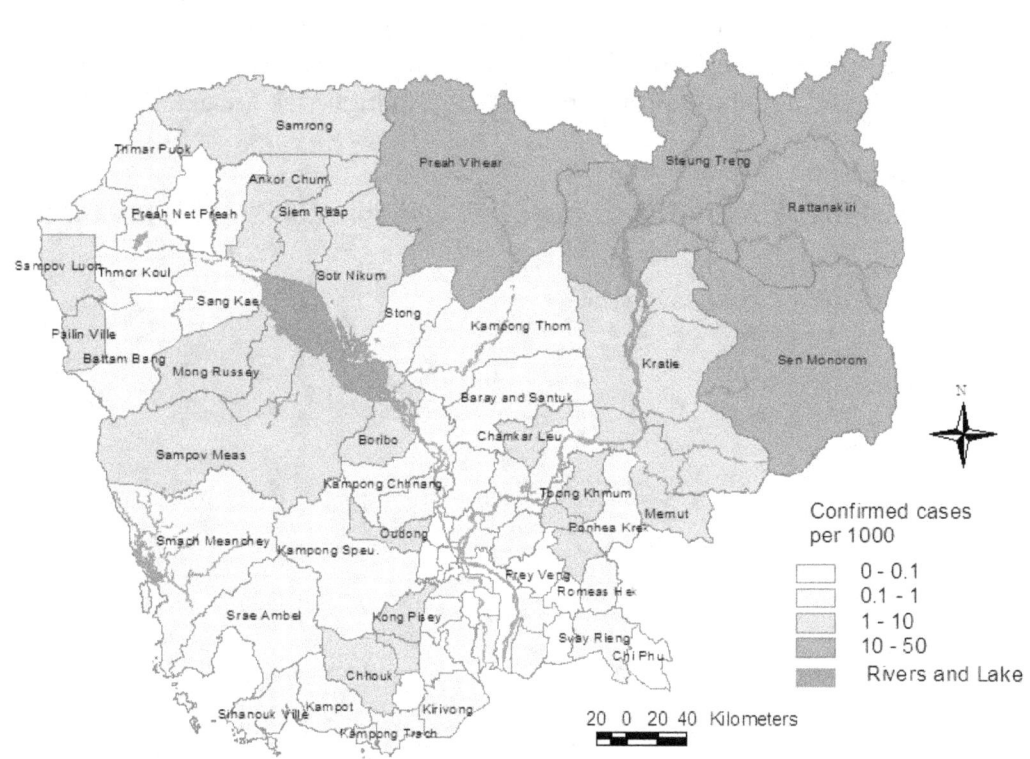

The national case management policy in Cambodia is to ensure access to quality diagnosis and treatment of positive cases with the ACT, DHA-piperaquine, which has been made available countrywide in public health facilities and through trained VMWs. In Cambodia, ACTs are used to treat both uncomplicated *P. falciparum* and *P. vivax* malaria infections. In response to the reduced efficacy of DHA-Pip in Pailin, the national treatment guidelines were revised in 2012 authorizing the use of Malarone® (atovaquone/proguanil) in that province. Unfortunately, molecular genotyping revealed the presence of atovaquone resistance mutations within six months of introduction, necessitating discontinuation of Malarone®, and reversion back to DHA-Pip. Despite documentation of successive TES demonstrating unacceptable DHA-Pip cure rates in four additional operational districts/provinces, the drug remains in use as there is no feasible alternative treatment available.

Cambodia's malaria burden continues to be disproportionately borne by ethnic minority groups, mobile, migrant, and cross-border populations, representing a huge challenge for prevention and control. Artesunate and other monotherapies can still be found in the unregulated private sector in Cambodia, despite efforts to ensure availability of high-quality ACTs and a ban on oral artesunate monotherapies. Certain sectors, such as the military, continue to use non-WHO pre-qualified antimalarials for first-line treatment.

2. Health system delivery structure and organization

CNM sits within the MOH. The leadership of the malaria control activities within Cambodia rests at the central level; however, with the decentralization of the MOH, Provincial Health Department (PHD) and Operational District (OD) malaria supervisors are involved with planning and implementing activities. VMWs, VHVs, MMWs, and local authorities help improve the availability and accessibility of malaria services, including early diagnosis and treatment, LLIN distribution, and malaria health education.

Figure 14: Organizational chart of the Ministry of Health, Cambodia (Source: MOH)

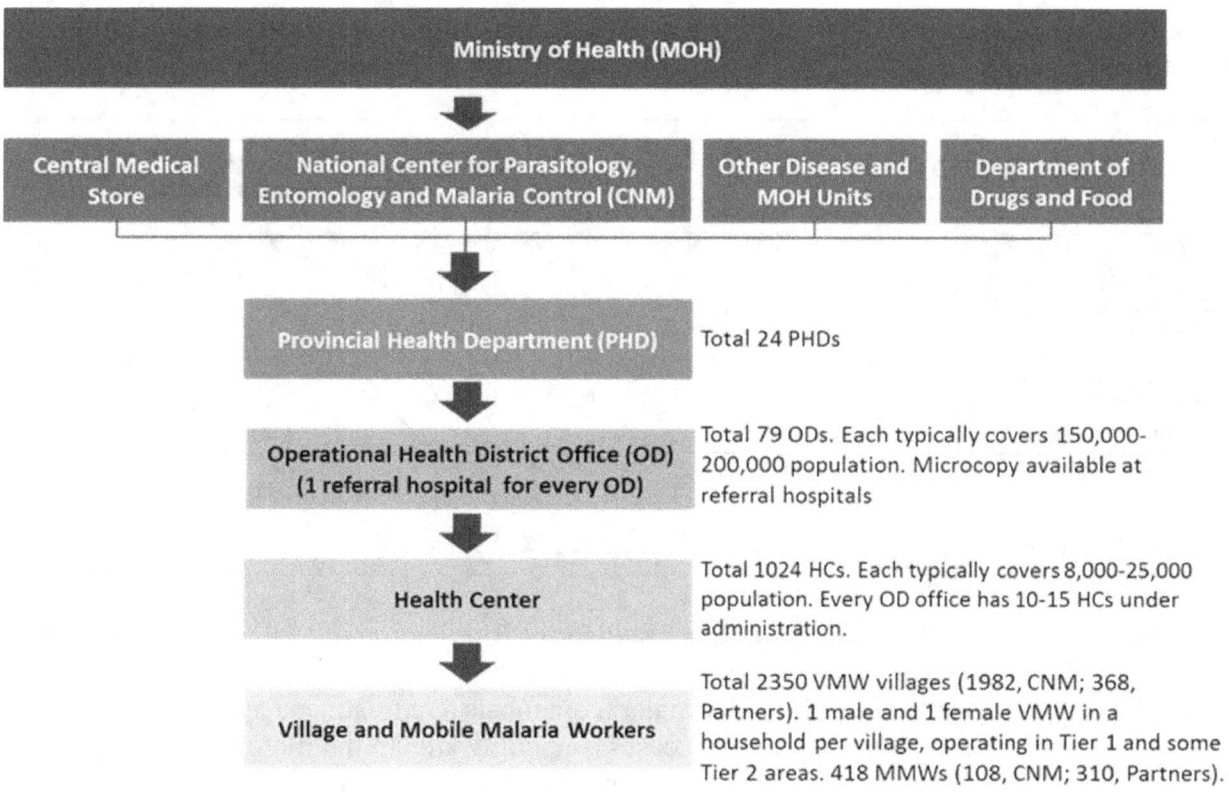

3. National malaria control strategy

Cambodia has drafted a new strategic plan following the Prime Minister's announcement that Cambodia will seek to eliminate malaria by 2025. This strategy, the National Strategic Plan for Elimination of Malaria, is based on the following goals:

- *Short-Term (by 2015)*
  To move towards pre-elimination of malaria across Cambodia with special efforts to contain artemisinin-resistant *P. falciparum* malaria.

- *Medium-Term (by 2020)*
  To move towards elimination of malaria across Cambodia with an initial focus on *P. falciparum* malaria and ensure zero deaths from malaria.

- *Long-Term (by 2025)*
  To achieve phased elimination of all forms of malaria in Cambodia.

Figure 15: Phased approach from malaria control to pre-elimination and elimination in Cambodia

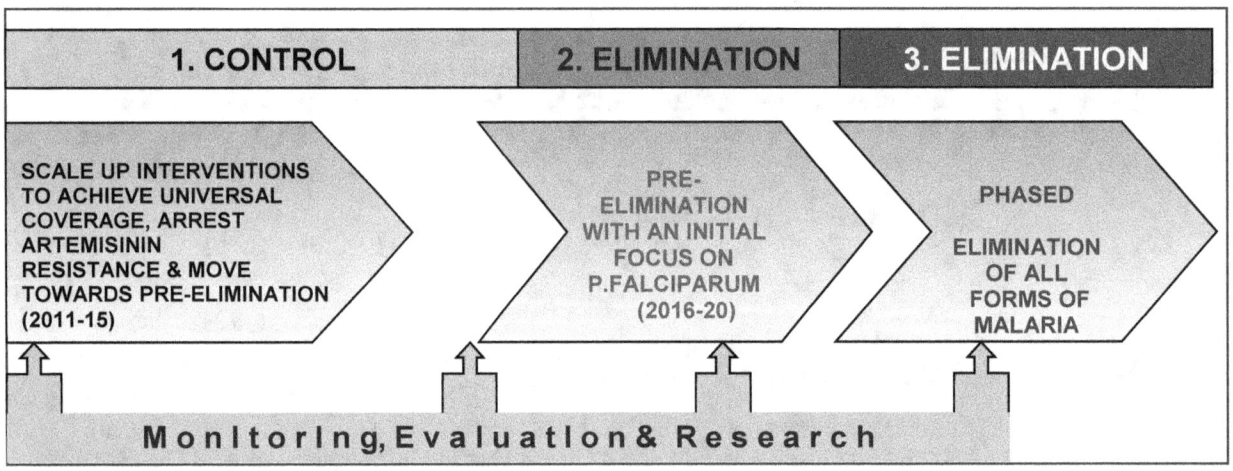

The strategic objectives of the National Strategic Plan for Elimination of Malaria are as follows:

1. To ensure universal access to early malaria diagnosis and treatment services with an emphasis on detection of all malaria cases (including among mobile/migrant populations) and ensure effective treatment including clearance of *P. falciparum* gametocytes and dormant liver stages of *P. vivax*.
2. To halt drug pressure for selection of artemisinin-resistant malaria parasites by improving access to appropriate treatment and preventing use of monotherapies and substandard drugs in both public and private sectors.
3. To ensure universal access to preventive measures and specifically prevent transmission of artemisinin-resistant malaria parasites among target populations (including

mobile/migrant populations) by mosquito control, personal protection, and environmental manipulation.

4. To ensure universal community awareness and behavior change among the population at risk and support the containment of artemisinin-resistant parasites and eliminate all forms of malaria through comprehensive BCC, community mobilization, and advocacy.

5. To provide effective management (including information systems and surveillance) and coordination to enable rapid and high-quality implementation of the elimination strategy.

During the implementation period covered by this strategic plan, Cambodia will need to transition from the malaria control to the malaria pre-elimination phase. In concert, PMI will support pilot elimination approaches in one OD, Sampov Loun, focusing on *P. falciparum* initially, as consistent with the NSP.

Revised National Treatment Guidelines/Policies:

The MOH has developed a revised version of the national treatment guidelines for malaria incorporating updated information presented at the national malaria drug policy meetings held in December 2013 and January 2014. The MOH set the following aims: 1) to further aggressively reduce malaria morbidity and mortality to reach malaria pre-elimination, 2) to reduce the impact of resistant malaria strains and preserve the current arsenal of malaria treatments by optimizing drug regimens and extending case management to follow up patients in high-risk areas to ensure successful cure, and 3) to promote more aggressive diagnostic testing to accurately diagnose and treat a larger proportion of malaria infections. To achieve these objectives, updates in the 2015 treatment guidelines include:

- Targeting DHA-Pip and artesunate-mefloquine for uncomplicated *P. falciparum* by province
- Replacing existing co-blistered artesunate-mefloquine with a fixed-dose combination
- Emphasizing DOT and ensuring clearance as an essential part of case management
- Enhancing timely surveillance to inform drug treatment policy
- Reduced primaquine dosing to block *P. falciparum* malaria in compliance with 2012 WHO guidelines on transmission and amending *P. vivax* radical cure dosing options.

4. Integration, collaboration, and coordination

Funding

The Global Fund has been the major donor for malaria control since 2005. The following Global Fund mechanisms are in place in Cambodia: SSF is ending in June 2015, RAI is ending in 2016, and the NFM (approximately $30 million total budget) will be implemented from July 2015 through December 2017 with UNOPs serving as the principal recipient for both grants. PMI is the second largest donor supporting malaria control and elimination activities in Cambodia. The BMGF is the third largest donor assisting CNM with the development of new tools to accelerate towards elimination and strategies to prevent infection and block transmission.

Table 18: Current malaria funding in Cambodia

Funding	Total Budget in USD (Funds Disbursed)	Duration	Key Implementing Partners	Key Activities
Domestic	3,484,029			Treatment services for Cambodian citizens (2012 Funding)
Global Fund SSF	50,953,325 (37,370,392)	2013-2015	CNM, UNOPS (PR)	Pre-elimination
Global Fund RAI	15,000,000	2014-2016	CNM, UNOPS (PR)	Artemisinin Resistance Containment
Global Fund NFM	30,000,000	2015-2017	UNOPS (PR)	Malaria control and prevention

5. Progress on coverage/impact indicators to date

Cambodia continues to make progress against malaria by continually enhancing approaches to reach key affected populations. Mass distribution of LLINs and LLIHNs has been implemented, particularly in the western part of the country that received much attention due to artemisinin resistance. During 2013, twelve malaria-related deaths were reported; a significant drop from 46 in 2012. The total number of malaria cases from public facilities and those treated by VMWs decreased to 44,632 cases compared to that of 74,541 one year earlier, representing a 42% reduction. Incidence of confirmed malaria decreased from 5 per 1,000 to 3 per 1,000, demonstrating progress towards elimination. The provinces with the highest numbers of malaria cases are Preah Vihear, Stung Treng, Ratanakiri, and Kratie. PMI is supporting efforts to diagnose and treat malaria cases seen by the private sector and incorporate these cases into national malaria data systems.

Since 2004, CNM has conducted nationwide malaria indicator surveys to measure the progress of the malaria program and to help the program make strategy and implementation shifts. These household and outlet malaria surveys provide useful trend information on key malaria indicators of malaria prevalence, ITN coverage and use, as well as treatment-seeking behaviors over time.

Table 19: Key indicators from the Cambodia Malaria Surveys (2004, 2007, 2010, and 2013)

Indicator	2004	2007	2010	2013
Malaria prevalence by microscopy (%)	4.4	2.6	0.9	0.1*
Households with at least one mosquito net (%)	95	100	99.4	99.7
Households with at least one ITN (%)	35.8	42.6	74.7	89.5
Persons who slept under an ITN the previous night (%)	29.3	25.3	52.6	59.6
Children under five years old who slept under an ITN the previous night (%)	26.4	28.0	56.3	63.3
Pregnant women who slept under an ITN the previous night (%)	13	N/A	59.1	61.5
% Women who received two or more doses of IPTp during their last pregnancy in the last two years	NA			

*1.5% prevalence by PCR

6. Challenges and opportunities

Challenges

Lack of efficacious first-line ACT treatments: In Cambodia, there remains no single ACT in widespread use which can be expected to produce efficacious cure rates at the desired WHO recommendation of >90%. In 2015, the MOH adopted new treatment guidelines which identify different first-line regimens by province in order to ensure the best possible cure rates. The feasibility of implementing a sub-national drug treatment policy is yet to be determined, but is certain to pose a logistical challenge, especially in community settings.

Private sector service delivery: As with many countries, self-medication and utilization of private outlets are the first choice for a sizeable proportion of the population seeking treatment for fever. To address this demand, PMI supports a "Public Private Mix" strategy in which registered private clinicians in the private sector are supported to ensure quality case management. PMI also supports a Quality Assurance System to assess and monitor these private providers' malaria case management skills and to ensure malaria data from the private sector are incorporated into Cambodia's Malaria Information System. USAID/Cambodia also supports a program to facilitate registration of private providers.

Limited malaria service delivery: Although some improvement has been made in the health care system, Cambodia still faces many challenges, such as decentralization and integration of malaria control into existing health care services, which places additional management burden on the provincial and district levels. Low salaries of government health staff result in limited public services. Village malaria workers who provide front line services in communities for early detection and treatment of malaria are covering many malaria-endemic parts of the country, but some lack supplies of RDTs and drugs, and receive insufficient support from district and provincial management.

Mobile and migrant populations: Cambodians pursuing economic opportunities in rice-cultivating areas and farming development projects often transit between non-malaria and malaria zones, unwittingly creating the potential for malaria transmission between them. These high-risk populations tend to be difficult to reach with health services. Increasingly, men (typically the occupational breadwinner) are moving with their spouse and their children to plantations, farms, development sites, and forested areas where access to public health facilities is limited. Hence, such populations may seek health care from private providers or pharmacies. Such outlets, and the medicines they stock, may be of dubious quality.

Integrating programs and limited human resources: Although the resource allocation for health from the Cambodian national budget has been increasing slowly, many infectious disease programs (such as malaria, TB, and HIV/AIDS) remain vertical and largely funded by external donors. Cambodia faces two issues: (1) sustainability and merging these vertical programs into the existing health system and (2) limited human resources and capacity in the health system. Particularly at district and health facility levels, there is shortage of skilled health professionals. Increased skills in key areas such as planning, implementation, monitoring, and evaluation will be critical as Cambodia moves from control to elimination.

Opportunities

Economic growth: Cambodia continues to enjoy rapid economic expansion among the countries in the GMS, with a 7% increase in gross domestic product (GDP) and a drop in the poverty rate to 17.7% in 2014. Cambodia achieved the Millennium Development Goal of halving poverty in 2009, and furthermore, the domestic budget has also seen an increase for the health sector.

Improving antenatal care and child health: Cambodia has made good strides in improving maternal and child health. The under-five mortality rate decreased from 124 per 100,000 live births in 2000 to 35 in 2014; and 95 percent of pregnant women who gave birth in the last five years received antenatal care at least once from a health professional (Cambodian Demographic Health Survey 2014).

(B) Operational Plan

1. Insecticide-treated nets

NMCP/PMI objectives

Cambodia's 2011-2025 National Strategic Plan for Elimination of Malaria calls for universal coverage and access to preventive measures among target populations, including mosquito control, personal protection and environmental manipulation, together with community awareness and behavior change among the population at risk. The strategy calls for one LLIN per person and one LLIHN per family provided for free to those living in villages at risk, as well as the retreatment of existing conventional nets with long-lasting insecticide. Nearly 3 million people, living less than 2 km from the forest edge, are targeted for LLINs and LLIHNs. Through a program supported by PMI, mobile and migrant populations receive one LLIN distributed either free or on loan from participating employers in high-risk zones, particularly plantations.

Cambodia has a strong "net culture." The Cambodia Malaria Survey from 2013 indicated that 99.7% of households owned at least one mosquito net and 80.3% had an ITN, but only 56.7% of all respondents reported sleeping under an ITN the previous night. The proportion who slept under an ITN the previous night was 59.6% for children under five years of age and 58.6% for pregnant women.

With an active and creative private market selling mosquito nets of various shapes, colors and sizes, Cambodian consumers seem to have developed particular preferences in the type of nets that they purchase and use. These preferences based upon the type of fabric (whether polyester or polyethylene), color, or size may also affect LLIN use. Anecdotal reports indicate that particular fabric types are preferred by Cambodians; however, this information is insufficient to allow the NMCP and the Global Fund to specify that LLINs with specific characteristics are to be procured.

Malaria transmission in highly endemic areas of the north and east must be lowered to reduce the number of migrants re-introducing malaria to low endemic districts endeavoring to eliminate malaria. With sufficient resources from the Global Fund in recent years to provide mass coverage of ITNs in high endemic areas throughout the country, PMI resources will be used strategically to fill gaps when necessary.

Progress since PMI was launched

Under the Global Fund Rounds 6 and 9 grants, the NMCP distributed 3,642,000 LLINs between 2011 and 2012. With the start of the Global Fund Round 9 grant implementation, a mass LLIN distribution campaign took place in early 2012, which covered 20 provinces (45

Operational Districts). These mass distributions of LLINs in Cambodia have resulted in increased proportion of households (all risk categories) with any LLINs (52% in 2010, 75% in 2013) and proportion with sufficient[1] LLINs (23% in 2010, 51% in 2013).

The majority of the distributed LLINs are procured by the Global Fund and distributed through periodic mass campaigns which mostly reach stable resident populations. PMI-procured LLINs are intended to fill gaps in PMI-target districts and to reach migrants and mobile populations. These gaps can arise if the district was not reached by the mass campaigns in which case a campaign-style distribution might occur. Most often, PMI LLINs are continuously distributed through community channels (e.g. village malaria workers, mobile malaria workers, plantation malaria workers, employers of migrants to reach high-risk populations without access to LLINs).

A PMI-supported rapid household net coverage assessment was conducted in 45 villages in May 2012 to measure the effectiveness of the LLIN distribution campaigns. Results showed that more than 95% of the LLINs expected to be distributed were indeed received at the household level. A shortage of LLINs at the health facilities was the main reason some households did not receive a LLIN during the campaign. Also, use of LLINs by permanent household residents (the night before the survey) was found to be very high (about 89%).

Progress during the last 12-18 months

With FY 2014 funds, PMI distributed 69,542 LLINs and LLIHNs to mobile and migrant workers. Among these, 43,647 and 25,895 LLINs were distributed through mass campaigns and through private/commercial sector channels, respectively.

---

[1] Sufficient LLINs is defined as at least 1 ITN/LLIN per 2 persons.

Commodity gap analysis

Table 20. Insecticide-treated Net (ITN) Gap Analysis

Calendar Year	2015	2016	2017
Total targeted population at risk*	8,988,000	9,122,820	9,259,662
Continuous Distribution Needs			
Continuous distribution	0	0	0
Mass Distribution Needs			
Mass distribution	848,942	861,676	878,932
Total Calculated Need**: **Routine and Campaign**	**848,942**	**861,676**	**878,932**
Partner Contributions			
ITNs carried over from previous year	-	39,345	0
ITNs from Global Fund (NFM)		735,000	945,000
ITNs from Global Fund (RAI)	818,745	-	
ITNs planned with PMI funding	69,542	83,000	60,000
Total ITNs Available	**888,287**	**857,345**	**1,005,000**
Total ITN Surplus (Gap)	**39,345**	**(4,331)**	**126,068**

*Calculated 8,600,000 + estimated 388,000 mobile population at risk (assumes 1.5% annual population growth rate)
** Total distribution need calculated as (population at risk * % households with sufficient nets per 2013 Cambodia malaria survey data)*1.8. Assumes replenishment of resulting gap over three years.

Plans and justification

PMI will continue to provide LLINs and/or LLIHNs to populations residing in malaria risk areas, including mobile and migrant workers. PMI will support distribution of LLINs to ensure high coverage in residual foci of transmission in elimination districts and will include a comprehensive approach for LLIN delivery which includes pre-distribution microplanning, interpersonal BCC messaging, and LLIN use monitoring and promotion at the household level.

Depending on the results of the formative phase of the net preference study, PMI will support a pilot study to compare use of different LLIN types to determine whether stated net preferences influence actual use. Since a large number of untreated nets are privately purchased in the GMS, PMI will identify barriers to LLIN use by targeted households and understand preferences that are appealing to consumers and associated with procurement decisions of commercially available nets to include: price, size, style (round/rectangular/hammock), denier (unit of fineness), privacy, color, insecticide treatment, and other factors.

Proposed activities with FY 2016 funding: ($650,000)

- **Procurement of LLINs and LLIHNs:** Procure approximately 60,000 LLINs and LLIHNs for target operational districts, incorporating preference data as appropriate to fill potential gaps, targeting migrant and mobile populations, and ensuring that residual foci of transmission in elimination areas are covered with LLINs. ($200,000)

- **Community-level support for distribution, promotion and use of LLINs:** PMI will utilize a comprehensive package for the distribution and delivery of LLINs, which includes pre-distribution micro-planning, and tailored BCC on the promotion and use of LLINs at the household level post-distribution by VMWs. The anticipated cost of LLIN distribution is approximately $1/ LLIN. ($200,000)

- **LLIN net preference study:** PMI will support a study to determine whether mosquito nets of a particular type of fiber are more or less likely to be used. The protocol will be informed by previously funded formative research and will be shared with the Global Fund to ensure that the type of evidence is sufficient to influence procurement policy. ($150,000)

- **LLIN durability monitoring:** PMI will support durability monitoring of LLINs, including assessment of physical durability and insecticide content, to inform future LLIN forecasting needs. ($100,000)

2. Malaria in pregnancy

NMCP/PMI objectives

In Cambodia, only 15% of all malaria cases are in women of reproductive age. Therefore, malaria during pregnancy is uncommon. When malaria does occur during pregnancy, though, there is an increased risk of severe disease in the mother and low birth weight and an increased risk of neonatal mortality in the newborn - similar to the risks that occur in higher prevalence settings.

Control of malaria in pregnancy and implementation of strategies in Cambodia are further complicated by heterogeneous transmission settings, transmission of both *P. falciparum* and *P. vivax*, and multi-drug resistant malaria. In addition, ANC attendance among pregnant Cambodian women could be improved. Overall, 89% of pregnant women attended ANC at least once, but only 27% of pregnant women attended the recommended four visits.

PMI support for preventing malaria during pregnancy focuses primarily on ensuring universal coverage of LLINs and providing appropriate messaging to ensure that pregnant women consistently sleep under a LLIN throughout their pregnancy. In addition, PMI has supported scaling-up of diagnosis and effective treatment of malaria at health facilities and through VMWs at community level, with particular targeting of migrant and mobile populations. National malaria treatment policies for pregnant women follow WHO recommendations: quinine is used in the first trimester and ACTs in the second and third trimesters. For severe malaria, quinine is recommended in the first trimester and artesunate or artemether in the second and third trimesters. Primaquine is contraindicated during pregnancy, but due to unavailability of reliable G6PD testing, currently no one receives primaquine. Because of the overall low prevalence of malaria during pregnancy, IPTp is not recommended.

Progress since PMI was launched

District-level campaigns supported by the Global Fund and PMI have resulted in high household LLIN ownership in all malaria-risk areas of Cambodia. With PMI support, almost one million interpersonal communication (IPC) encounters have been conducted to encourage regular use of LLINs.

In addition, approximately 800 facility health workers and VMWs per year undergo refresher training in malaria case management, which includes specific guidance on management of malaria in pregnant women.

Progress during the last 12-18 months

There are limited data to describe the burden of malaria among pregnant women in Cambodia. To better assess burden, PMI conducted a rapid assessment by instituting malaria screening at 13 ANCs across three provinces in differing malaria risk areas of Cambodia (Pursat, Battambang, and Mondulkiri). Test positivity rates in all three ODs were less than one percent, with almost half of all those women found to be infected presenting with symptoms of malaria. Based on these results, intermittent screening and treatment for pregnant women in antenatal settings has not been recommended for scale-up since it is more likely that pregnant women will seek care in community settings rather than in antenatal clinics. PMI will focus efforts on ensuring that specific content covering malaria in pregnancy is included in all its case management training activities.

In FY 2014, PMI supported the distribution of almost 70,000 LLINs and the insecticide retreatment of 12,785 traditional bed nets, although records are not kept on how many of these nets were provided to households with pregnant women.[1] In addition, almost one million IPC encounters were conducted encouraging regular LLIN use.

During FY 2014, in addition to filling gaps in ACTs and RDTs in ten targeted ODs, PMI supported refresher training for 808 facility health workers and VMWs in malaria case management, including the management of malaria in pregnant women, and training in malaria diagnosis (microscopy or RDTs) for 865 health workers and VMWs.

Commodity gap analysis

IPTp is not implemented in Cambodia. Therefore, SP is not required.

---

[1] Data from the 2010 Demographic and Health Survey indicate that approximately 5% of rural women of reproductive age are pregnant at any point in time.

Plans and justification

PMI will continue to support LLIN distribution to pregnant women, IPC to encourage LLIN use, and training and supervision of health workers and VMWs in malaria case management, which includes specific training in the management of malaria in pregnancy.

Proposed activities with FY 2016 funding: ($0)

- **LLIN distribution and promotion:** PMI will continue to support distribution of LLINs and IPC for pregnant mothers to promote LLIN use through district-level campaigns, in coordination with the Global Fund. (see ITN and BCC sections)

- **Strengthen case management of malaria in pregnancy:** Support will continue for training of facility health workers and VMWs in malaria diagnosis and treatment, including specific guidance on the treatment of malaria during pregnancy. (See Case Management section)

3. Case management

Diagnosis and treatment

NMCP/PMI objectives

In line with national policy, almost all malaria cases diagnosed at public sector facilities are confirmed by microscopy, or in some cases multi-species RDTs. At community level, VMWs are trained to perform multi-species RDTs to diagnose malaria and guide treatment. Malaria surveillance data indicates that almost all suspected malaria cases are confirmed by diagnostic testing. With the scale-up of VMWs, an increasing percentage of malaria cases are diagnosed at the community level. Of the total 56,271 malaria cases diagnosed in Cambodia in 2014, 29,993 (53.3%) were diagnosed by VMWs/MMWs.

Patients with confirmed malaria receive treatment either at health facilities or from VMWs/MMWs. After a VMW confirms that a patient has malaria using an RDT, they provide the first dose of treatment under direct observation and then follow-up patients to ensure they complete the three days of treatment. During the visit by the VMW to the patient on the third day, VMWs will inquire whether the patient took their treatment on Day 1 and Day 2 and ask to see the empty blister pack. In areas of known resistance, VMWs also have been trained to prepare a blood slide for microscopy on Day 3. In PMI-supported areas, directly observed therapy is provided and VMWs visit patients to ensure adherence on Day 1 and Day 2.

Because of increasing rates of treatment failures to DHA-Pip in some parts of Cambodia, particularly in the western and northern provinces, and genetic evidence of resistance (i.e. cytochrome b mutations) developing to atovaquone-proguanil in Pailin (where it was the first-line treatment), CNM updated the national malaria treatment policy in 2015. The new policy recommends reintroduction of artesunate-mefloquine in areas where treatment failures to DHA-

Pip and atovaquone-proguanil have been identified; and continuation of DHA-Pip in areas where treatment failures have not been identified. This policy will be implemented once artesunate-mefloquine has been procured and delivered to the country. Furthermore, the policy recommends more rigorous application of DOT and Day 3 follow-up, particularly in areas of known treatment failures.

Progress since PMI was launched

PMI has provided limited support to fill gaps in RDT and ACT requirements that are not covered by the Global Fund or government resources. The primary focus of PMI's support for case management has been on refresher training and routine supervision of both health facility workers and VMWs/MMWs in target areas. In addition, PMI has supported the implementation of a community supply system linked to health facilities, close monitoring of diagnostic stock levels at operational division warehouses, reinforcing and strengthening logistic management at the peripheral level, and maintenance of buffer stocks of laboratory commodities in PMI-targeted areas.

With PMI support, 606 VMWs have been trained and are providing malaria diagnosis and treatment services in targeted villages in 11 ODs. Training and supervision also has been provided to clinical and laboratory staff at 196 health facilities. Day 3 testing of malaria cases is being carried out by 426 VMWs in 14 health facility catchment areas.

PMI also provides support for quality assurance and case reporting to a network of registered private sector providers, in small clinics and drug shops that have been trained and provided with subsidized RDTs and ACTs with support from the Global Fund. Use of RDTs in these outlets has increased significantly since their introduction.

Progress during the last 12-18 months

In FY 2014, 6,000 atovaquone-proguanil tablets were procured with PMI funding and distributed to targeted health facilities in Pailin. More than 800 facility health workers and VMWs were trained in malaria cases management, including the use of RDTs. Another 57 received refresher training in malaria microscopy. With PMI support, 80 health facilities have a malaria microscopy QA system in place and 96 facilities received quarterly technical supervision visits.

In PMI-supported ODs, almost 96,000 malaria diagnostic tests were performed, with 46% being diagnosed by VMWs. Of these, 18,263 were treated for malaria, most (63%) by VMWs.

PMI also provided support for four clinical supervisors, who conducted 134 quality assurance visits to Global Fund-supported private providers, who offer malaria diagnosis with RDTs and treatment with quality-assured ACTs. This supervision is currently being scaled-up to all 454 private providers in this network. A DHIS2-based database was developed which collects case reports from these providers and also has a standardized checklist that the supervisors use during their visits.

PMI's support for therapeutic efficacy studies in Cambodia are described below in the "Surveillance: Drug resistance and therapeutic efficacy studies" section. Briefly, DHA-Pip efficacy testing at four sites in 2013-2014 showed ACPR >90%, but Day 3 positive rates ranged from 13-44%. Three sites in 2014-2015 assessed DHA-Pip efficacy: Siem Reap with 38% ACPR and 50% Day 3 positives; Stung Treng with 69% ACPR and 13% Day 3 positives, and Mondulkiri with 90% ACPR and 25% Day 3 positives.

Commodity gap analysis

Table 21: RDT Gap Analysis

Calendar Year	2015	2016	2017
RDT Needs			
Target population at risk for malaria	8,988,000	9,122,820	9,259,662
Total number projected fever cases	1,218,948	1,237,232	1,255,791
Percent of fever cases confirmed with microscopy	0.19	0.3	0.5
Percent of fever cases confirmed with RDT	0.81	0.7	0.5
Total RDT Needs	**987,348**	**866,063**	**627,895**
Partner Contributions			
RDTs carried over from previous year	-	205,152	-
RDTs from Global Fund NFM	500,000	555,039	141,131
RDTs from Global Fund RAI	407,000	-	-
RDTs planned with PMI funding	285,500	0	110,000
Total RDTs Available	**1,192,500**	**760,191**	**251,131**
Total RDT Surplus (Gap)	**205,152**	**(105,872)**	**(376,764)**

*Calculated 8,600,000 + estimated 388,000 mobile population at risk; assumes 1.5% annual population growth
** Projected fever cases includes estimated private sector cases; assumes 1.5% annual population growth

Table 22: ACT Gap Analysis

Calendar Year	2015	2016	2017
ACT Needs			
Target population at risk for malaria*	8,988,000	9,122,820	9,259,662
Total projected number of malaria cases	46,314	43,940	41,466
Total ACT Needs**	**94,017**	**89,198**	**84,176**
Partner Contributions			
ACTs carried over from previous year	39,689	163,649	198,391
ACTs from Global Fund SSF	152,897	-	-
ACTs from Global Fund NFM	-	103,940	91,466
ACTs from Global Fund RAI	46,800	-	-
ACTs planned with PMI funding	18,280	20,000	50,000
Total ACTs Available	**257,666**	**287,589**	**339,857**
Total ACT Surplus (Gap)	**163,649**	**198,391**	**255,681**

*Calculated 8,600,000 + estimated 388,000 mobile population at risk; assumes 1.5% annual population growth
** Includes buffer stock, a small contingency for possible outbreaks or upsurge in cases, and the potential shift in treatment-seeking away from the private sector to the public sector; assumes 1.5% annual population growth

The new Global Fund grant, under NFM, provides support for 100% of all projected ACTs through 2017 and RDT requirements through 2016. PMI FY 2016 funds will be used to procure 110,000 RDTs to fill part of the anticipated 2017 gap for RDTs. It is anticipated that the next Global Fund grant will cover the balance, but the funding levels post-2016 have not yet been determined. As has been done in previous years, PMI allocates very limited support to fill unanticipated gaps in ACTs that might result from incorrect quantifications, unexpected upsurge in fever/malaria cases, or delays in procurement of Global Fund commodities.

Plans and justification

PMI will continue support for diagnostic testing and clinical case management at facility and community level in targeted ODs in Cambodia, including provision of commodities to fill gaps, and refresher training and supervision of health facility staff and VMWs. This support will include intensified case management activities in target elimination ODs.

Proposed activities with FY 2016 funding: ($1,865,000)

- **Procure RDTs and microscopy supplies:** PMI will procure multi-species RDTs, microscopes, and reagents and supplies for microscopy to fill gaps in country requirements, particularly for migrant and mobile populations. This will include approximately 110,000

RDTs, which will cover one-quarter of the anticipated gap in 2017. The remaining gap should be covered by the next Global Fund grant. ($75,000)

- **Procure ACTs:** PMI will procure approximately 50,000 ACT treatments to fill gaps not already filled by Global Fund and domestic resources. ($50,000)

- **Private sector quality assurance:** PMI will continue support for supervision and case reporting of a network of registered private providers. ($400,000)

- **Training, supervision, and quality assurance of malaria diagnosis and treatment at facility and community levels.** PMI will support its network of VMWs/MMWs and health facilities in targeted ODs, which will include refresher training and supervisory visits. PMI also will continue support for quality assurance of malaria diagnosis at targeted health facility laboratories. ($1,300,000)

- **Evaluation of the implementation of the sub-national drug treatment policy**: PMI will evaluate the feasibility and implementation of Cambodia's sub-national treatment guidelines to inform development of future treatment guidelines. This assessment will primarily involve a management assessment of the implementation of this policy to determine the feasibility of implementing different treatment policies in different parts of the country. It will include assessment of the supply chain, drug availability, and treatment practices of health workers. ($40,000)

Pharmaceutical management

NMCP/PMI objectives

Effective malaria case management requires that efficacious, high-quality antimalarials are available and used by both public and private providers and patients according to national treatment guidelines. The Central Medical Store is responsible for distributing essential medicines and medical commodities to PHDs and ODs on a quarterly basis. The supplies that arrive at the OD stores are primarily purchased with national budget and donor funds. These goods are stored in the OD warehouses and then distributed to health facilities based on a "pull" system; when requests are received from the HC, the OD provides medical commodities based on these requests when they have the requested drugs in stock. If the OD store is severely overstocked with a particular commodity, some OD stores will resort to a "push" system to help rebalance their inventory levels. Cambodia's Central Medical Store will also resort to "push" policies if it has commodities on its shelves that are nearing six months until expiry. Oversupply and undersupply do occur at health facility and community levels.

Malaria diagnostics and treatment services are free in public health facilities, thus malaria medicines are also provided free of charge. However stockouts at health facilities sometimes result in patients purchasing medicines in the private sector. This creates a barrier to malaria treatment, which disproportionately affects the poor.

Progress since PMI was launched

PMI continues to monitor regional malaria commodity pipelines, so potential bottlenecks in procurement and distribution of malaria commodities (including Global Fund-financed commodities) can be quickly addressed. PMI has supported a regional logistics advisor to provide technical assistance on supply chain management issues and manage regional procurements. The regional technical advisor provided information on malaria commodity pipelines for the region, analyzed potential gaps and weaknesses, as well as supported various supply chain management activities on behalf of partners.

Progress during the last 12-18 months

A preliminary assessment was conducted on data and commodity flows from village to central level to assess the availability and quality of data from Cambodia's LMIS. The assessment concluded that the Drug Inventory Database (DID), a component of the LMIS, was a fairly robust system. At the health center level, staff use paper forms while at the OD level, data are entered into an automated district database that feeds into a national database. Despite this, information cannot be accessed in a systematic way and used by key decision-makers at national level. For example, while malaria commodity stock on hand and consumption data are entered into the DID at each level of the system, CNM only has access to quarterly data aggregated by OD. Hence, CNM cannot trace commodity data to sub-district level individual health facilities, hindering efforts to identify and mitigate shortages and stockouts of malaria commodities for end users. PMI plans to update the DID system to provide timely information for programmatic decision-making, and in so doing, leverage other USG efforts to assist Cambodia in developing better supply chain management systems across various health programs.

Stockouts and unavailability of ACTs has been the result of procurement constraints or lack of access or availability of consumption data. Restricted access to data on stock levels of malaria commodities throughout the supply chain system, and the lack of a standardized methodology for quantification of commodity needs limit CNM's ability to forecast malaria commodity needs and develop a supply plan based on actual stock levels. This also affects donor procurements to be able to ensure that an adequate number of commodities are forecasted and procured.

To remedy this, PMI supported a two-day logistics quantification overview workshop in 2015. The workshop focused on strengthening CNM staff capacity in the use of malaria forecasting data and methods, and supply planning concepts and tools. As a result of the workshop, PMI has been requested to plan for technical assistance to conduct a national quantification exercise for malaria commodities with CNM and malaria partners.

Plans and justification

To address the above-mentioned shortcomings, PMI will provide further support to CNM in assessing and developing a more efficient LMIS system that provides timely information on malaria commodities and strengthens the ability to forecast and quantify malaria supply needs.

Proposed activities with FY 2016 funding: ($150,000)

- **Support for pharmaceutical management and logistics:** PMI will monitor and address potential bottlenecks in procurement and distribution of malaria commodities (including Global Fund-financed commodities) to ensure timely availability of RDTs, laboratory supplies, and antimalarials in target areas, as well as to respond to urgent requests. The technical support will focus on supply chain strengthening, forecasting, quantification, management, and distribution of pharmaceuticals and RDTs. ($150,000)

Drug quality

NMCP/PMI objectives

To address the issue of counterfeit goods, the Cambodian government recently established a new national Counter Counterfeit Committee, a cross-sectoral task force comprised of representatives from the Ministries of Interior, Justice, Health Finance, Commerce, and Defense. This national Committee was publicly launched on November 2014 and dedicated to combatting counterfeit products with an adverse impact on public health and safety in Cambodia. In January 2015, the Counter Counterfeit Committee facilitated the development of a joint action plan between Cambodian Ministries of Interior and Health centered on performing inspections in private markets to detect and combat counterfeit medicines and to regulate private pharmacies and providers to ensure delivery of quality medicines and pharmaceutical services for the Cambodian population.

A recent study of antimalarial quality in Cambodian outlets[1] illustrated a mixed picture with respect to drug quality. The study analyzed drugs purchased from retail outlets, categorizing as "acceptable" quality, "falsified (fake drugs which do not contain the stated active pharmaceutical ingredient or API)" or "substandard (genuine medicines produced by authorized manufacturers which do not have the correct amount of API)". Although no falsified drugs were detected, substandard drugs were found in 31% of the Cambodian samples. These findings, reassuring for the absence of "falsified" drugs, nonetheless cause the Cambodian government great concern as "substandard" drugs can also imperil the safety of malaria patients and contribute to the future development of antimalarial resistance across drug classes.

The Global Fund supports the Department of Drugs and Food (DDF) to eliminate banned oral artemisinin monotherapies, combat counterfeit and substandard malaria drugs through sample screening at public and private pharmacies, and strengthen the national pharmacovigilance system. Many of these activities, while focused on malaria, will also help to ensure access of quality-assured essential medicines for TB, HIV/AIDS, and other health priority programs.

Progress since PMI was launched

---

[1] Yeung, et al. Am J Trop Med Hyg **2015** 14-0391

PMI continues to support the Cambodian MOH to monitor antimalarial drug quality and to take action when falsified or substandard medicines are found. PMI worked closely with the DDF and other local partners to ensure that Minilab® reference standards were replenished and that regulatory authorities continued to make routine drug inspections and field visits. With assistance from PMI, the DDF successfully launched raids on facilities selling unregistered and falsified antimalarial medications. Additionally, to ensure a continuous stream of professionals aware of the problem with substandard and falsified medicines, PMI supported the updating of QA/QC and medicine regulations curriculum for Cambodian pharmacy and medical students.

Progress during the last 12-18 months

With PMI support, the DDF's National Health Products Quality Control Center's (NHQC) laboratory is developing a draft of their quality manual and standard operating procedures needed to support ISO certification and continues to collect antimalarial drugs through pharmaceutical outlets that can be used to train NHQC personnel throughout the ISO certification process. PMI also supported the NHQC's participation in an Asia-Pacific inter-laboratory quality assurance program.

Plans and justification

Previous PMI drug quality objectives in Cambodia have spanned three objectives: Improving detection of poor-quality medicines and supporting the MOH to take action against counterfeit and substandard medicines and health products based on the results of post-marketing surveillance testing; strengthening medicines QA/QC through building the capacity of the DDF and NHQC; and raising awareness about medicines quality issues and improving access to medicines quality information among regulators, health care professionals, and the general public.

One of the highest priorities of the DDF's pharmaceutical sector strategic plan of action 2013-2018 is to support the NHQC to implement its roadmap towards the attainment of ISO 17025 certification by 2017. Future PMI support will focus on supporting the NHQC in its pursuit of ISO certification.

Proposed activities with FY 2016 funding: ($128,000)

- **Drug Quality Assurance:** PMI will provide technical assistance to the NHQC laboratory to achieve international standard ISO 17025 certification. ($128,000)

4. Health system strengthening and capacity building

PMI supports a broad array of health system strengthening activities which cut across intervention areas, such as training of health workers, supply chain management and health information systems strengthening, drug quality monitoring, and NCMP capacity building. PMI supports VMWs as critical extensions of the public health system and critical to treatment of malaria cases at the village level – where the burden of disease remains highest. Another important component of the health system is the vast private sector, where PMI supports quality improvement and quality of services.

NMCP/PMI objectives

The MOH's Second Health Strategic Plan (HSP2) 2008 – 2015 identifies three priority program areas and five cross-cutting health system strategies. The three priority program areas include: maternal, neonatal, and child health; communicable diseases (including HIV, TB, and malaria); and non-communicable diseases. The five health system strategies include: health service delivery; health care financing; human resources; health information systems; and health system governance. A new strategic plan, HSP3, is currently under development and is expected to start in 2016. In support of HSP2, NMCP's 2010 – 2025 Strategy sets an ambitious agenda of eliminating all forms of malaria by 2025. To reach these goals, the NMCP will build the capacity of community and facility-based health care workers to actively find malaria cases and improve case management while strengthening linkages with the private sector. In addition, the NMCP will need to strengthen surveillance and information systems to meet the need for real-time data to support an elimination strategy.

PMI works in close partnership with CNM to build capacity in the form of technical assistance and training to CNM, PHD, and OD staff. Although some improvements have been made in the health care system, Cambodia still faces many challenges, such as decentralization and integration of malaria control into existing health care services, placing additional management burden on provincial and district levels. Low salaries of government health staff results in limited public services. Village malaria workers who provide front-line services in communities for early detection and treatment of malaria are covering many malaria-endemic parts of the country, but receive insufficient support from district and provincial management. In addition, quality of care with regard to diagnostics and treatment face many challenges in both the public and private sectors.

PMI's capacity building efforts are also complemented by broader health systems strengthening activities using other USG funding. For example, USAID is also providing technical assistance: to implement and expand Cambodia's social health protection scheme; to strengthen the HMIS; to support the MOH in licensing and registration of private healthcare providers; and to develop new health financing approaches. All USAID and PMI-supported health systems work is in line with the MOH's HSP2 and alignment with HSP3 will also be assessed starting in 2016.

Progress since PMI was launched

PMI has supported health systems strengthening activities at the VMW, health facility, private provider, CNM, PHD, and OD levels.

At the community level, PMI has supported training and skills strengthening of VMWs in performing multi-species RDTs to diagnose malaria and provide correct treatment. In addition, PMI has supported the implementation of a community supply system linked to health facilities, close monitoring of diagnostic stock levels at operational division warehouses, reinforcing and strengthening logistic management at peripheral level, and maintenance of buffer stocks of laboratory commodities in PMI-targeted areas.

At the health facility level, QA systems for microscopy have been established with regular supervision visits. PMI has also provided support for quality assurance and case reporting for a network of private sector providers. At PHD and OD levels, PMI also supports the development of annual operations plans that promote government ownership of health activities at lower levels of the health system and are used to plan, coordinate, and monitor malaria and other health activities at sub-national level.

With regard to drug efficacy, TES study execution emphasizes quality diagnostics, and builds CNM's capacity to conduct proper research techniques, such as protocol development and adherence to regular study monitoring and quality assurance practices.

PMI also takes a hands-on approach through technical assistance in field entomology, emphasizing training in vector bionomics, monitoring of insecticide resistance, and assessment of LLIN durability.

Progress during the last 12-18 months

In February 2015, PMI supported a two-day quantification overview workshop focused on strengthening CNM staff capacity in the use of malaria commodity forecasting data and methods, and supply planning concepts and tools. As a result of the workshop, PMI has been requested to plan for technical assistance to conduct a national quantification exercise for malaria commodities with CNM and malaria partners. PMI also provided technical assistance to DDF on plans to establish an ISO-certified drug quality testing lab that would provide the country with the capacity to ensure drug quality in the country.

PMI has also continued to support capacity building of malaria program managers and staff through in-country trainings and workshops, joint supervision visits, and international courses. PMI has also established a provincial-level working group on malaria elimination in selected provinces which will serve as a platform for stakeholder coordination on elimination activities. PMI also rolled out a quality assurance system and tools to improve the quality of malaria diagnosis and care in the private sector. Over 400 private providers have been assessed so far.

Plans and justification

PMI will continue to work closely with CNM to identify and fill capacity gaps. Such discussions have identified needs in technical areas such as enhancing M&E, developing capacity to effectively implement various aspects of malaria control and elimination, enhancing CNM's capacity to effectively coordinate malaria stakeholders, and manage malaria tools and reports generated by CNM partners (such as Standard Operating Procedures and study reports). Health systems strengthening activities are implemented through relevant PMI core technical areas, with the aim of strengthening CNM capacity in various aspects of diagnosis and case management, supply chain and logistics, quality improvement, and M&E.

Proposed activities with FY 2016 funding: ($100,000)

- **Management capacity building:** PMI will support CNM and targeted ODs and PHDs to strengthen their capacity in program and supply chain management and monitoring and evaluation. ($100,000)

Table 23: Health Systems Strengthening Activities

HSS Building Block	Technical Area	Description of Activity
Health Services	Case Management	• PMI will continue support for supervision and case reporting of a network of private providers who are supported by the Global Fund. • PMI also will continue support for quality assurance of malaria diagnosis at targeted health facility laboratories.
Health Workforce	Case Management BCC	• Build, through training and technical assistance, a cadre of CHWs/VMWs to properly diagnose, treat, and report on malaria cases into the public health system. This will include refresher training and supervisory visits. Additional training to be added for treatment of malaria during pregnancy. • New communication tools, materials, and job aids will be developed for health care providers to help improve acceptance and implementation of elimination activities around diagnosis, case investigation, and treatment. Interpersonal communication for each patient will also be tailored to specific risk behaviors of individual patients, households, and villages.
Health Information	Pharmaceutical Management & Logistics Monitoring and Evaluation	• The logistics management information system will be modernized to provide real-time data to decision-makers and avoid stockouts. • The malaria information system will be updated to a web-based system.
Essential Medical Products, Vaccines, and Technologies	Pharmaceutical Management & Logistics	• PMI will monitor and address potential bottlenecks in procurement and distribution of malaria commodities (including Global Fund-financed commodities). Technical support will focus on supply chain strengthening, forecasting, quantification, management, and distribution of pharmaceuticals and RDTs.
Leadership and Governance	Elimination	• PMI will strengthen sub-national committees (PHDs/ODs) to manage elimination activities in target ODs.

138

5. Behavior change communication

NMCP/PMI objectives

In Cambodia, BCC and social mobilization efforts play a crucial role in reaching hard-to-reach populations, which are often at the highest risk of malaria. High-risk populations include residents of forested areas, new settlers, internal migrant workers, and people crossing border areas. Currently there is a BCC Working Group that is organized and chaired by CNM. In support of the National Elimination Plan 2011-2025, CNM through this working group launched a "National Behavior Change Communication Strategy for Malaria Elimination in Cambodia" in 2013. The key objectives of the BCC interventions in this strategy are to increase consistent use of ITNs among target communities, improve health-seeking behaviors among at-risk populations, improve compliance with medication, and increase awareness of risks related to artemisinin monotherapies. With increased mobility within and beyond national boundaries, the above strategy outlines components specific for mobile and migrant populations that focuses on providing tailored BCC interventions to migrants at four stages/settings: 1) where they live prior to migration, 2) *en route* along the migration path, 3) at arrival points, and 4) at cross-border areas.

Progress since PMI was launched

PMI has supported several innovative approaches targeting mobile migrant populations, including tailored mass media, messaging through taxi drivers around migrant corridors, as well as strengthening cross-border collaboration. Malaria awareness campaigns targeting local residents, mobile seasonal workers, and people traveling into endemic areas have been conducted through various channels for reinforcement. Travelers into endemic zones receive and discuss malaria prevention issues and messages with trained malaria volunteers at key transit points and taxi drivers participating in the program. VMWs and MMWs provide counseling and treatment services to patients in villages, at farms, and plantations. PMI also trains registered pharmacists and drug sellers in cities and towns on diagnostic testing and rational drug use.

Progress during the last 12-18 months

With FY 2014 funding, PMI intensified BCC efforts around IPC, building upon successes of prior years. As of April 2014, 226,838 individuals were educated through IPC. In addition, 108 villages across 9 provinces conducted World Malaria Day Activities. As PMI moves towards pre-elimination activities in Sampov Loun, BCC activities will be streamlined and focus less on control efforts across large geographic areas. A variety of BCC materials were produced for VMWs, mobile and migrant populations, and health care providers including posters, leaflets, flipcharts, stickers, t-shirts, banners, bags, signboards, billboards, etc., in multiple languages. Early diagnosis and treatment and interpersonal communication was provided by 125 health facilities and 865 VMWs/MMWs.

As of April 2015, 606 VMWs/MMWs have been trained and provided outreach and IPC to patients and at-risk populations in target provinces and districts reaching 48,249 mobile and migrant workers. Among them were 24,269 women, of which 477 were pregnant. Various forms of "infotainment" have been employed to capture the attention of rural populations. Mobile malaria video shows and malaria quizzes, provided along with testing and treatment services, were presented in 98 endemic villages. During these activities, 3,854 people were tested and 131 were treated after testing positive for malaria.

A folk play group was engaged to perform live community theatre to bring malaria stories and key messages to rural low-literate audiences in forested areas. The group performed 12 sessions to over 4,160 spectators. In a province in the northeast where children under 15 years old constitute 50% of malaria patients, PMI supported training of 41 primary school teachers on malaria transmission, malaria parasites, signs/symptoms, care-seeking behaviors, and malaria prevention so that they can continue teaching schoolchildren to prevent and seek appropriate malaria treatment. At border areas in the west, to which Cambodians travel for work, PMI supported the provision of materials in the Khmer language explaining malaria services in Thailand and possible side effects from malaria treatment. PMI has also supported semi-annual meetings between Cambodian and Thai health authorities along border provinces to discuss harmonization of bilingual BCC materials and to share malaria information about cross-border migrant populations. It is anticipated that information-sharing will continue with local resources.

PMI is currently initiating efforts with FY 2014 funds to assess current net use and preferences to guide donors' LLIN procurement and retreatment policy. Since a large number of untreated nets are privately purchased in the GMS, PMI will identify barriers to LLIN use.

Plans and justification

As Cambodia is moving from malaria control to elimination in certain ODs, with FY 2016 funding PMI will focus BCC efforts and messages to serve control and elimination goals. BCC interventions will focus increasingly on supporting elimination efforts, including: developing targeted BCC messages specific to the highest risk migrant groups within elimination ODs and increasing acceptance of reactive/active case detection efforts. A multi-pronged, comprehensive approach for BCC interventions will be implemented to sustain community involvement and support, promote health behaviors, and reduce risk-taking in the context of malaria exposure. New communication tools, materials, and job aids will be developed for health care providers to help improve acceptance and implementation of elimination activities around diagnosis, case investigation, and treatment. IPC will also be tailored to specific risk behaviors of individual patients, households, and villages.

Proposed activities with FY 2016 funding: ($150,000)

- **BCC community-level implementation in target areas:** PMI will support development and implementation of effective BCC approaches for target elimination and control ODs. Careful consideration will be given to training of health workers and VMWs and tailoring of BCC messages according to identified risk factors. PMI will assist CNM to identify those risk factors and to refine approaches in support of the National BCC Strategy. In elimination areas, BCC efforts will also focus on increasing acceptance of reactive/active case detection in the context of declining infections. In control areas, PMI will continue supporting BCC activities (IPC & media) to reach the highest risk groups by focusing on improving coverage and use of malaria prevention measures (LLINs, LLIHNs), increasing awareness of malaria in pregnancy, dangers of counterfeit antimalarials, as well as ensuring prompt diagnosis and effective treatment. ($150,000)

6. Monitoring and evaluation

NMCP/PMI objectives

Cambodia's 2011-2025 National Strategic Plan for Elimination of Malaria has set a national goal to eliminate all forms of malaria by 2025. CNM prioritizes data collection through a variety of methods, including routine program monitoring, baseline, mid-term, and end-line quantitative and qualitative surveys. Cambodia relies on the Health Management Information System (HMIS) to collect data from public health facilities throughout the country. In addition, a parallel malaria information system (MIS) has been developed to capture malaria case load data from health facilities and VMWs/MMWs in malaria-endemic areas. Data from the HMIS is currently automatically extracted and incorporated into the MIS to provide a complete picture of the malaria burden in the country. However, similar to many other countries, neither the HMIS nor MIS include malaria data routinely collected from the private sector.

Within each OD, health centers are classified as high or low transmission based on cumulative three-year incidence. Artemisinin-resistant *P. falciparum* is found in nine provinces and is the basis for the current system of stratification based on two tiers: Tier 1 being those nine provinces with demonstrated artemisinin resistance; and Tier 2 referring to the other 11 provinces that, by definition, are at risk but where resistance has not been confirmed.

Based on this stratification, the total population at risk in Cambodia is 8.6 million persons. The Global Fund SSF grant covers 3.3 million people in 45 ODs (living within the catchment area of 340 health centers) and RAI covers the remaining 5.3 million. An estimated mobile population of 388,000 also contributes to the total population at risk.

Cambodia has conducted longitudinal national malaria household surveys in 2004, 2007, 2010, and 2013. These data have shown decreasing malaria prevalence by microscopy and increasing ITN coverage and use.

Table 24: Monitoring and Evaluation (Surveys conducted or planned in Cambodia)

Data Source	Survey Activities	Year								
		2009	2010	2011	2012	2013	2014	2015	2016	2017
Household surveys	Demographic Health Survey (DHS)*		X				X			
	Malaria Indicator Survey (MIS)*		X			X				
Malaria Surveillance and Routine System Support	Support to malaria surveillance system					X	X	X	X	X
	Support to HMIS*					X	X	X	X	X
Therapeutic	*In vivo* efficacy testing	X	X	X	X	X	X	X	X	X
Entomology	Entomological surveillance and resistance monitoring				X	X	X	X	X	X

*Not PMI funded

Progress since PMI was launched

PMI has supported routine malaria surveillance data collection at the community level, provided technical support for household malaria surveys, surveillance system strengthening, and TES since its inception in the GMS. As part of its case management activities, PMI also works with CNM personnel to build capacity and ensure that malaria data from case management activities, such as number of tests conducted and malaria cases diagnosed by VMWs are captured by the health centers and ODs. PMI has worked closely with medical and public health personnel from the provincial level to the community level to collect, verify, and analyze monthly malaria data by village.

For routine case reporting, PMI supported CNM's MIS that incorporates health facility and community-level malaria data reported by village malaria workers. This system was designed to include relevant program data (e.g., bed net distribution, malaria drug and diagnostic stock, and listing of private sector providers) and link to the national health information system.

Progress during the last 12-18 months

In an effort to improve data flow from communities to the central level, PMI has begun working with CNM to assess alternative web-based surveillance platforms designed for real-time malaria surveillance.

Since the malaria surveillance data underestimates the true burden with the majority of malaria treatments occurring in the private sector, PMI has begun to engage with private sector providers to develop a system of malaria case reporting. To improve collection of data from migrants and mobile populations, a cadre of MMWs has been deployed and their malaria data are now incorporated into the malaria surveillance system.

Plans and justification

As CNM implements its national elimination strategy, access to timely malaria information becomes critical. As malaria cases decrease, PMI will work with CNM to ensure rapid reporting of malaria cases, initiate timely case investigation and response activities, including reactive surveillance, and to eliminate transmission foci. WHO recommends that the API be less than one before the transition to elimination begins, but the actual API will depend on financial resources and the ability of personnel to track cases. To accommodate this, PMI will continue to support the strengthening of the malaria information system to enable better malaria surveillance in endemic areas as well as increase its support for surveillance in elimination areas.

Proposed activities with FY 2016 funding: ($503,000)

- **Support for M&E activities and surveillance strengthening**: Support will be provided in revising national strategic plans as well as updating national M&E plans. Technical assistance will be provided to ensure quality routine surveillance and survey data collection have been harmonized with other regional efforts. Efforts will focus on incorporating data from the private sector and mobile and migrant populations. PMI will support CNM in coordinating their M&E work stream. ($183,000)

- **Private sector malaria data collection:** PMI will provide targeted support to improve case management quality assurance activities in the private sector, as well as implementing a reporting system to capture malaria confirmed case information, which will eventually be incorporated into the Cambodian national malaria surveillance system. (see Case Management section)

- **Support for enhanced surveillance and M&E in elimination settings:** PMI will pilot China's "1-3-7" elimination approach in elimination ODs, which entails rapid reporting of malaria cases within one day, confirmation and case investigation within three days, and a follow-up response within seven days. This activity will also include costing and evaluation of elimination-specific activities, and be scaled up if shown to be feasible and cost-appropriate. ($300,000)

- **Technical assistance with M&E:** Two CDC TDYs are planned to provide technical assistance for M&E. ($20,000)

7. Surveillance: Drug resistance and therapeutic efficacy studies

NMCP/PMI objectives

With global and regional concern for artemisinin resistance, a regional TES monitoring network was formed with USAID support in 2000. Since 2011, PMI has continued to support the regional network which includes sentinel sites in Cambodia. While artemisinin resistance continues to be confined to certain hotspots in the GMS, TES remains crucial in informing Cambodia's national drug policies. With limited efficacious first-line treatments available in Cambodia, CNM is conducting efficacy testing of artesunate-pyronaridine (Pyramax®) in Pailin and Pursat and is preliminarily noting acceptable Day 28 cure rates.

Progress since PMI was launched

In Cambodia, 11 sentinel sites, alternating every other year, conduct drug efficacy monitoring of first-line and second-line treatments for both *P. falciparum* and *P. vivax*. The PMI-supported TES network first alerted the global community about the potential emergence of artemisinin resistance in Pailin. Since 2008, the Day 3 positive rate for those treated with DHA-Pip in both Pailin and Pursat provinces, in North-west Cambodia, bordering Thailand have been higher than 10% indicating reduced drug efficacy. Based on these studies, the treatment policy in Cambodia was changed in 2008 to DHA-Pip. Now, with increasing evidence of reduced efficacy of DHA-Pip to *P. falciparum*, the national drug policy was updated again in 2015.

Progress during the last 12-18 months

CNM convened two international consultations attended by various subject matter experts on drug resistance in December 2013 and January 2014 to develop guidance for the national drug policy. Studies by the US NIH, AFRIMS, and PMI demonstrated reduced cure rates against DHA-piperaquine. Specifically, adequate clinical and parasitological response for *P. falciparum* of <90% in Pailin, Battambang, Pursat, Oddar Meanchey, and Preah Vihear were noted as shown in Figure 16.

Figure 16: PMI and non-PMI-supported therapeutic efficacy study sites in Cambodia (2009-2013) (Source: Cambodia National Treatment Guidelines, 2015, MOH)

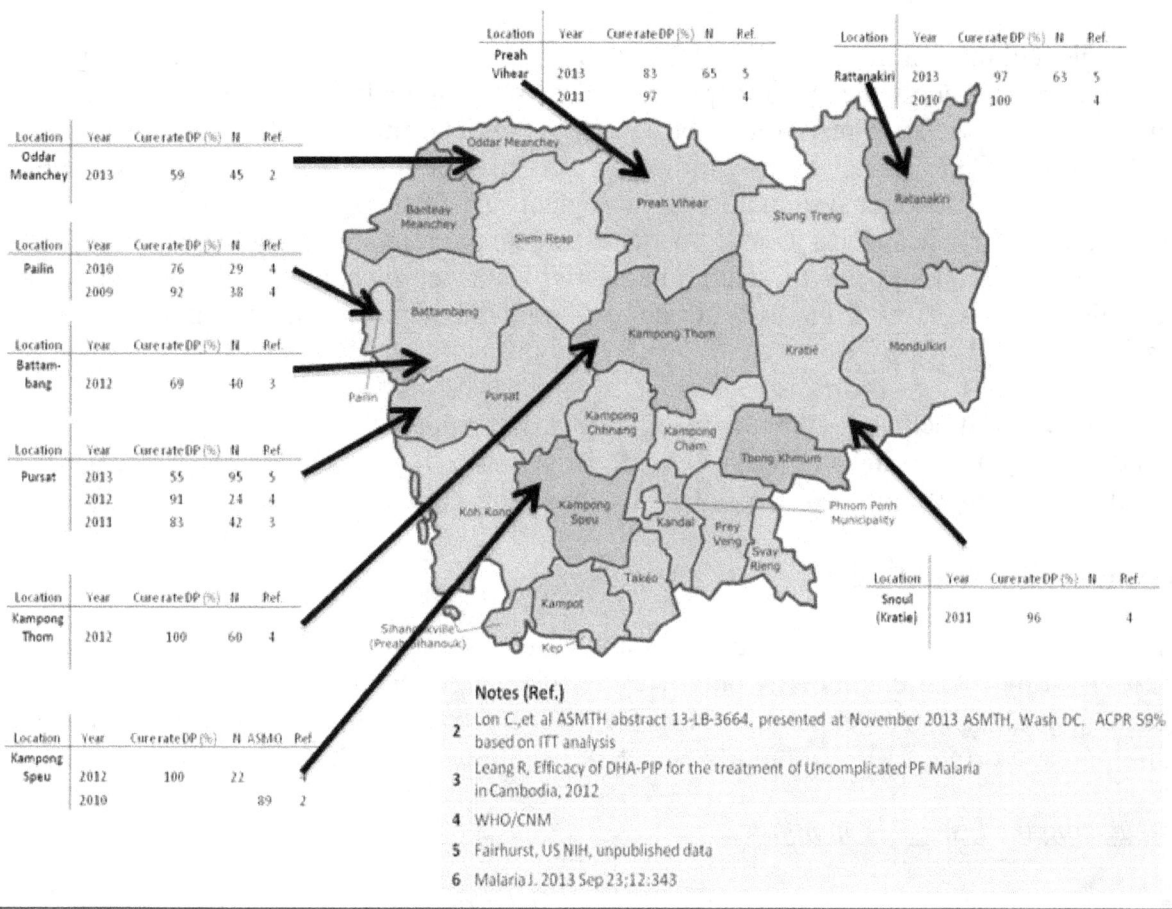

In 2015, PMI supported CNM's therapeutic efficacy studies in Kampot, Preah Vihear, Kratie, and Rattanakiri provinces. Preliminary plans for 2015-2016 are to conduct therapeutic efficacy studies of DHA-Pip in Siem Reap, Stung Treng, and Mondulkiri provinces.

Plans and justification

With FY 2016 funding, PMI will continue to support 11 alternating sentinel sites for monitoring first and second-line therapies in Cambodia.

Proposed activities with FY 2016 funding: ($270,000)

- **Cambodia TES:** In Cambodia, PMI will support in-country TES sites, technical assistance, monitoring, and supervision from a WHO investigator, and biannual TES meeting. Support for molecular surveillance of K13 and other key drug resistance polymorphisms will also be provided. ($270,000)

8. Surveillance: Entomology

NMCP/PMI objectives

CNM has indicated that entomological surveillance of three types are needed: 1) Surveillance to determine malaria risk and which vector species are transmitting malaria, 2) Surveillance to determine levels of insecticide resistance, and 3) Testing to determine insecticide activity of LLINs. At present, CNM carries out entomological surveillance in collaboration with research groups, but it does not conduct systematic entomological surveillance of any type, largely because of staff limitations. CNM seeks to better elucidate the relationship between vector bionomics, especially biting behavior and human activities (sleeping habits, movement patterns, night activities, net usage, etc.), and to better understand the dynamics of indoor and outdoor transmission.

Given the heavy investment of Cambodia in LLIN procurement and distribution, there is a need for LLIN durability monitoring and for systematic surveillance for insecticide resistance in the most important malaria vectors in the country, *An. dirus* and *An. minimus*.

Progress since PMI was launched

PMI has supported PMI partners to conduct entomologic surveillance in Cambodia via collaboration with CNM's entomology unit. Key activities have centered on periodic vector surveillance in Pailin and Battambang provinces. PMI has provided direct technical assistance and training in sporozoite ELISA antibody detection techniques to build CNM's capacity.

Progress during the last 12-18 months

Last year, one CNM staff member participated in a PMI-supported training in Burma in use of the bottle bioassay and WHO tube test. She has subsequently trained one technician in the technique. However, no systems for surveillance of resistance, insecticide content in LLINs via bioassays, or entomological risk have been developed in Cambodia. This has been identified by CNM and PMI as a priority for the country. CNM has a functioning insectary, funded by the NIH, which houses colonies of mosquitoes for parasitological research.

Plans and justification

With FY 2016 funding, PMI will focus on monitoring LLIN durability including residual insecticide activity in distributed LLINs and insecticide resistance monitoring in sentinel sites.

Proposed activities with FY 2016 funding: ($179,000)

- **Insecticide resistance monitoring:** PMI will support field collections to allow surveillance for insecticide resistance in high endemic areas of the country. ($150,000)

- **Technical assistance with entomology:** A CDC entomologist will provide technical assistance to build entomologic capacity for insecticide resistance and LLIN durability monitoring. ($29,000)

9. Operational research

NMCP/PMI objectives

Although all GMS countries are expected to provide radical treatment for *P. vivax*, only China and Thailand widely use primaquine. Most countries with concerns of severe variants of G6PD deficiency lack testing capacity at the peripheral level and do not provide primaquine therapy. WHO now recommends that a single dose of 0.25mg/kg primaquine can be given to patients with *P. falciparum* to reduce transmission without G6PD deficiency testing[1]. However, Cambodia's guidelines specify that primaquine should be given to confirmed malaria patients for *P. falciparum* transmission-blocking[2] and *P. vivax* radical cure only if G6PD status is known. To assist CNM in deploying primaquine for both applications, PMI will support CNM by conducting a pair of studies. The first study ("Tolerability and safety of low-dose primaquine for transmission blocking in symptomatic *falciparum*-infected Cambodians") will assess the hematological response of administering low-dose primaquine in G6PD-deficient subjects. The second study will assess the validity and feasibility of deploying G6PD RDTs to health facility and community levels to facilitate the use of higher doses of primaquine for radical cure of *P. vivax*.

Progress since PMI was launched

PMI supported an evaluation of a third-generation point-of-care RDT to assess for G6PD deficiency. Such a point-of-care test that could safely guide treatment with primaquine both for the clearance of *P. falciparum* gametocytes as well as for the prevention of relapses by *P. vivax* will have tremendous programmatic implications. The third generation RDT had high sensitivity in detecting G6PD enzymatic activity of <30% comparable to the fluorescent spot test, the current laboratory standard[3]. This information confirmed the potential use of the product for use in radically curative regimens for *P. vivax* malaria.

Progress during the last 12-18 months

In 2015, enrollment began for the "Tolerability and safety of low-dose primaquine for transmission blocking in symptomatic falciparum infected Cambodians" study. If proven safe,

---

[1] WHO Policy Brief on single-dose primaquine as a gametocytocide in *P. falciparum* malaria, January 2015
[2] It is recognised that WHO now recommends that a single dose of 0.25mg/kg primaquine can be given to patients with *P. falciparum* to reduce transmission without G6PD deficiency testing (WHO Policy Brief on single-dose primaquine as a gametocytocide in *P. falciparum* malaria, January 2015) However, Cambodia's guidelines recommend testing, reflecting concerns related to the high prevalence of G6PD deficiency.
[3] Field Trial Evaluation of the Performances of Point-of-Care Tests for Screening G6PD Deficiency in Cambodia, A. Roca- Feltrer et al; PlosOne, 2014

data obtained from this study will provide CNM the evidence to widely implement this globally recommended strategy to target *P. falciparum* gametocytes. In addition, the study entitled "Feasibility of deploying G6PD RDTs to health facility and community levels" has received conditional approval from Cambodia's national ethics board and is planned to begin in mid-2015.

Table 25: PMI-funded operational research studies

Completed OR Studies				
Title	**Start date**	**End date**	**Budget**	**Justification**
Test performance of the CareStart G6PD RDT	January 2013	December 2013	$100,000	Initial evaluation of newly marketed test to screen for G6PD deficiency
Ongoing OR Studies				
Title	**Start date**	**End date**	**Budget**	**Justification**
Tolerability and safety of low-dose primaquine for transmission blocking in symptomatic *falciparum*-infected Cambodians	February 2015	June 2016	$150,000	Assists CNM in decision to deploy low-dose primaquine as part of national policy
Feasibility of deploying G6PD RDTs to health facility and community levels	October 2014	October 2015	$150,000	Evaluates feasibility of deploying the G6PD RDT in field settings
Planned OR Studies with FY 2016 funding: None				

Plans and justification

There are no planned OR studies with FY 2016 funding.

10. Staffing and administration

One health professional will serve as the resident advisor to oversee PMI in Cambodia and represent USAID. In addition, two resident advisors based in RDMA, one representing CDC and one representing USAID, provide periodic technical support. In addition, two Foreign Service Nationals (FSNs), one based in Cambodia and one in RDMA, also work as part of the PMI Cambodia team. All PMI staff members are part of a single interagency team led by the USAID Mission Director or his/her designee in country. The PMI team shares responsibility for development and implementation of PMI strategies and work plans, coordination with national authorities, managing collaborating agencies and supervising day-to-day activities. Candidates for the resident advisor position (whether initial hires or replacements) will be evaluated and/or interviewed jointly by USAID and CDC, and both agencies will be involved in hiring decisions, with the final decision made by the individual agency.

The PMI professional staff work together to oversee all technical and administrative aspects of PMI, including implementing malaria prevention and treatment activities, monitoring and evaluation of outcomes and impact, reporting of results, and providing guidance to PMI partners.

The PMI lead in country is the USAID Mission Director. The day-to-day lead for PMI is delegated to the USAID Health Office Director and thus the PMI resident advisor reports to the USAID Health Office Director for day-to-day leadership, and works together as a part of a single interagency team. The technical expertise housed in Atlanta and Washington guides PMI programmatic efforts.

The PMI resident advisor is based within the USAID health office and is expected to spend approximately half his/her time sitting with and providing technical assistance to the national malaria control programs and partners.

Locally-hired staff to support PMI activities either in Ministries or in USAID will be approved by the USAID Mission Director. Because of the need to adhere to specific country policies and USAID accounting regulations, any transfer of PMI funds directly to Ministries or host governments will need to be approved by the USAID Mission Director and Controller, in addition to the US Global Malaria Coordinator.

Proposed activities with FY 2016 funding: ($505,000)

- Salary, benefits and travel for Cambodia USAID/PMI Resident Advisor. ($300,000)

- Salary, benefits and travel for Cambodia FSN. ($100,000)

- Administrative and programmatic support from USAID/Cambodia, including contracting, financial management, program, and health office cross-cutting support. ($90,000)

- Travel costs for RDMA-based USAID/PMI Resident Advisor and FSN. ($15,000)

Table 1: Budget Breakdown by Mechanism

President's Malaria Initiative – *Cambodia*

Planned Malaria Obligations for FY 2016

Mechanism	Geographic Area	Activity	Budget ($)	%
TBD	Targeted areas	a) Case management at community level, including implementation, training, and supervision; b) Training and supervision for microscopy; c) BCC technical assistance for community-level implementation; d) M&E and surveillance strengthening; e) Capacity building for in-country coordination	$3,073,000	68%
TBD - Supply Chain Contract	Targeted areas	Procurement of LLINs, LLIHNs, RDTs, and ACTs; supply chain strengthening	$475,000	11%
WHO Consolidated Grant	Selected sites	Conduct TES (including PfMDR and K13 analysis) to inform treatment policy	$270,000	6%
CDC IAA	National	Technical support for entomology (2 TDYs) and M&E (2 TDYs)	$49,000	1%
TBD	National	Support to strengthen national laboratory for drug quality monitoring	$128,000	3%
USAID	National	Salary costs for one Resident Advisor and Foreign Service National, administrative and program costs, and travel costs for RDMA-based staff	$505,000	11%
Total			**$4,500,000**	**100%**

Table 2: Budget Breakdown by Activity

President's Malaria Initiative – *Cambodia*

Planned Malaria Obligations for FY 2016

Proposed Activity	Mechanism	Budget Total $	Budget Commodity $	Geographic Area	Description
PREVENTIVE ACTIVITIES					
Insecticide-treated Nets					
LLIN/LLIHN procurement	TBD - Supply Chain Contract	$200,000	$200,000	5-8 Operational Districts	Support for approximately ~60,000 LLINs and LLIHNs (hammocks) for focus areas, filling potential gaps, and targeting migrant and mobile populations
Community level distribution and promotion of ITNs	TBD	$200,000		5-8 Operational Districts	Support of a comprehensive package for distribution of LLINs (approximately $1/LLIN), including pre-distribution micro-planning, tailored BCC on the promotion and use of LLINs, and LLIN monitoring at household level post-distribution by VMWs
Net preference study	TBD	$150,000		Selected sites	Longitudinal study to determine user net preferences to inform procurement policies and practices
LLIN durability monitoring	TBD	$100,000		Selected sites	Durability monitoring of LLINs (incl. physical durability and insecticide content) to inform timing of future LLIN procurements
Subtotal ITNs		$650,000	$200,000		
Indoor Residual Spraying					
Subtotal IRS		$0	$0		
Malaria in Pregnancy					
Subtotal Malaria in Pregnancy		$0	$0		
SUBTOTAL PREVENTIVE		$650,000	$200,000		
CASE MANAGEMENT					
Diagnosis and Treatment					

151

Activity	Description	Geographic Area			Mechanism
Procurement of RDTs	~110,000 RDTs and microscopy supplies procured for focus areas for use by community level health volunteers with expansion to new operational	5-8 Operational Districts	$75,000	$75,000	TBD - Supply Chain Contract
Procurement of antimalarial drugs	Procure ~50,000 ACTs or other first-line treatment for use by community level health volunteers or workers; targeting migrant and mobile populations and to fill commodity gaps in public and private sector.	5-8 Operational Districts	$50,000	$50,000	TBD - Supply Chain Contract
Quality assurance of case management in the private sector	Improve quality of private sector case management through medical detailing, monitoring and supervision; provision of malaria data to national surveillance system	5-8 Operational Districts		$400,000	TBD
Case management at the community level, including implementation, training and supervision	Training and supervision of community-based malaria case management activities both broadly and in relation to malaria elimination; includes specific case management practices for malaria in pregnancy	5-8 Operational Districts		$1,300,000	TBD
Evaluation of implementation of sub-national drug treatment policy	Evaluation of feasibility and implementation of subnational Cambodia NTGs to inform development of future treatment guidelines	Selected sites		$40,000	TBD
Subtotal Diagnosis and Treatment			$125,000	$1,865,000	
Pharmaceutical Management					
Supply chain strengthening	Strengthening the pharmaceutical management systems, forecasting, quantification, management and distribution of pharmaceuticals and RDTs. Emphasis on country-specific technical assistance for supply chain strengthening.	National		$150,000	TBD - Supply Chain Contract
Drug Quality Assurance	Support for DDF laboratory to reach ISO certification.	National		$128,000	TBD
Subtotal Pharmaceutical Management			$0	$278,000	
SUBTOTAL CASE MANAGEMENT			$125,000	$2,143,000	
HEALTH SYSTEM STRENGTHENING / CAPACITY BUILDING					
Capacity building for in-country coordination and management	Capacity building for CNM and PHDs/ODs to support oversight and management of control and elimination activities			$100,000	TBD
SUBTOTAL HSS &			$0	$100,000	

CAPACITY BUILDING					
BEHAVIOR CHANGE COMMUNICATION					
BCC community-level implementation	TBD	5-8 Operational Districts	$150,000		Support for developing and implementing effective BCC approaches for control and intensified approaches for elimination activities (e.g., early detection and treatment of individual cases, conducting case notification, investigations, timely responses to cases, strategies to educate malaria patients on the importance of case follow-up and regimen adherence, etc.)
SUBTOTAL BCC			$150,000	$0	
MONITORING AND EVALUATION					
M&E strengthening	TBD	National	$183,000		Build capacity at CNM/PHD/OD level to collect, analyze and use data; transition to DHIS2 platform, including software development and training.
Enhanced surveillance and M&E in elimination settings	TBD	5-8 Operational Districts	$300,000		Support for implementing case-based, real-time reporting system in elimination ODs, including training and use of electronic reporting. Includes costing of elimination-specific activities
CDC technical assistance for M&E	CDC IAA	National	$20,000		Two TDYs for M&E support
Therapeutic efficacy surveillance studies	WHO consolidated grant	Selected sites	$270,000		For TES implementation costs and PfMDR and K13 or other genetic marker testing to support drug policy decisions
Entomology surveillance and vector control	TBD	Selected sites	$150,000		Focus on increasing capacity and range of surveillance for insecticide resistance
CDC technical assistance for entomologic surveillance	CDC IAA	National	$29,000		Two TDYs for entomologic support and LLIN durability monitoring support
SUBTOTAL M&E			$952,000	$0	
OPERATIONAL RESEARCH					
SUBTOTAL OR			$0	$0	
IN-COUNTRY STAFFING AND ADMINISTRATION					
USAID RA Cambodia	USAID		$300,000		One RA salary cost
USAID FSN Cambodia	USAID		$100,000		One FSN salary cost
Cambodia Mission support	USAID		$90,000		Mission administrative costs
RDMA FSN and RA travel	USAID		$15,000		Technical assistance travel from RDMA staff

153

SUBTOTAL IN-COUNTRY STAFFING	$505,000	$0	
GRAND TOTAL	**$4,500,000**	**$325,000**	

154